WHEN
JOHNNY
CAME
MARCHING
HOME

WHEN JOHNNY CAME MARCHING HOME

MIKE BERRY

THE CHOIR PRESS

First published in the United Kingdom in 2023 by

The Choir Press

ISBN 978-1-78963-384-9

Contents

Note to Reader

It is important to point out that this book in no way reflects on the Japanese nation subsequent to World War Two. This story is a graphic description of how thousands of men and women suffered at the hands of the Imperial Japanese Army under the control and orders of Emperor Hirohito and the Imperial High Command. The events are true and the atrocities committed happened and should never be forgotten.

Dedication

This book is dedicated to all the deceased FEPOW heroes, survivors and also their family and friends who all suffered too in one way or another.

'They shall grow not old, as we that are left grow old
Age shall not weary them, nor the year's condemn
At the going down of the sun and in the morning
We will remember them'

God Bless Them All 🙏

BUCKINGHAM PALACE

The Queen and I bid you a very warm welcome home.

Through all the great trials and sufferings which you have undergone at the hands of the Japanese, you and your comrades have been constantly in our thoughts. We know from the accounts we have already received how heavy those sufferings have been. We know also that these have been endured by you with the highest courage.

We mourn with you the deaths of so many of your gallant comrades.

With all our hearts, we hope that your return from captivity will bring you and your families a full measure of happiness, which you may long enjoy together.

George R.I

September 1945.

Preface

This book is a graphically detailed account of a brutal and violent period of recent history that highlights a frenzied cult-like behaviour by one nation's army, which in this case was the Imperial Japanese Army countenanced by their Imperial High Command and, ultimately, Emperor Hirohito. The atrocities referred to actually happened, and the Japanese nation paid a very heavy price for their futile attempt to achieve global domination at any cost.

Many other nations have committed similar atrocities—if not worse—in the past that were equally as horrible, but most have since developed and become more civilised in their ways.

It is important that subsequent generations are informed of these atrocities so that they understand that similar situations must never be repeated. Most civilised nations teach the full history of their past in school curricula.

Johnny and his fellow prisoners' tragic story should be a cautionary warning to all nations that while warfare is virtually inevitable, the codes of conflict should always be adhered to as laid down in the agreed conventions of war, particularly with reference to prisoners and civilians. Failure to do so results in a heavy price being paid, which should serve as a deterrent. Unfortunately, though, history is littered with many barbaric acts of man's inhumanity to man, which I truly hope and pray we have seen the last of. But alas, I fear not.

However ultimately this book is an enlightening and inspirational account of the fortitude, bravery and conduct of a young ordinary soldier.

His survival depended on his extraordinary mental strength, determination and will power.

But probably the most important reason for his survival was the stoical spirit and camaraderie of his fellow captives who helped him through this horrific ordeal.

The Story is based on numerous lengthy conversations with Johnny and people who knew him well, including family members, friends and fellow FEPOWs, own accounts of Japanese barbarity.

He never had the chance or inclination to tell the story of his ordeal at the hands of his captors so I am proud and honoured to write it for him.

CHAPTER ONE

STREETS OF LIVERPOOL

Liverpool was a bleak, dirty city in the 1920s and 1930s, due to the intense concentration of thick black soot produced by all the domestic coal fires and heavy industry that poured out across the port skyline. The sloping streets of Toxteth were filled with a multitude of vivid raucous noises, the predominant ones being the clanking of passing trams on the lines, the rattling of horse-drawn carts on the cobbled streets, the cries of the coalmen, the shouts of the rag-and-bone men, paperboys chattering, factory shift hooters and the ships' horns tooting loudly and dominantly from the nearby River Mersey.

The ubiquitous lamplighter rode around the streets on his old bike at dusk to light the gas street lamps with his long pole. The ornate metal lampposts were popular gathering points for the local kids to meet and play around at night, the most favourite pastime of all being swinging from them, in the yellow glow of the gaslight, using a knotted rope tied to the bar on top. This was as good and enjoyable as any of the rides at the fairground, and the kids would keep themselves amused with it for hours on end.

In this impoverished era of the Great Depression, life in this underprivileged area was extremely difficult for the many large, struggling working-class families. There was mass unemployment, abject poverty, slum housing and general deprivation, but the local kids would still go out and play happily from morning till night, finding so many things to do and to play with. Most parents had no idea where their children were, but most escaped any serious harm and returned home late in the day with just a few bumps and grazes, if anything.

Schooling was compulsory from 5 years of age till 14, when most children left to enter the workplace or stay home to help out with their younger siblings; families tended to be much larger in those days.

There were many roaming gangs of unruly juvenile tearaways in the south end of Liverpool, none more notorious than the infamous 'Peanut Gang'. They committed an assortment of crimes, including assault, intimidation, street robberies and robbing sailors and soldiers passing through the port. Youngsters walking to and from school were easy targets and often fell foul of their violent attacks.

Johnny would not join the gangs, as he could look after himself well enough in these sorts of confrontations. He was just under 14 in 1930 and one day was on his way home from school with his younger brother Joe. As they approached the corner of Upper Stanhope Street and Park Road in Toxteth, Liverpool 8, where they lived, there was a gang of four older, scruffy, rough-looking scallywags loitering about waiting for them. They started to pick on Joe and asked the brothers to empty their pockets. They began mocking and teasing them in a most aggressive and nasty manner. The leader of the gang was a particularly mean, offensive boy, who ridiculed young Joe to his face, calling him a big cissy and suchlike.

An explosive short right hook from Johnny connected firmly on the startled bully's chin, placing him painfully on his backside on the cobbled street. The others instantly backed away in shock, apart from one, who tried his luck with a lurching swing with a bottle ... which missed. Another explosive punch from Johnny placed him swiftly on the ground too.

Johnny said nothing and calmly picked up Joe's cap and handed it to him, and they silently made their way up the street to their old, run-down Victorian slum dwelling. His growing reputation made similar skirmishes few and far between from them on.

Johnny lived with six brothers, Mum (Emily), Dad (John) and Aggie, his younger sister, plus a few cats, which kept the rodent level down.

The old decrepit house stood close to and in the shadow of the majestic and imposing Gothic Anglican Cathedral, ranked as the fifth tallest in the world and being one of the world's tallest non-spired church buildings. Its construction began in 1904 and was only completed in 1978, having luckily suffered only superficial damage in 1941 during the devastating Blitz. It was truly a magnificent and impressive structure, proudly dominating the skyline of the city and visible from many miles away. The grandeur of this palatial cathedral was in stark contrast to the surrounding poverty-stricken area of slum houses, where there was mass unemployment in what was a booming port. (The wealthy merchants inhabited other quarters of the city). However, it was a great adventure playground for the local children, with the enticing cavernous surroundings in the extensive grounds providing many places to hide and play. Sir John Betjeman once called it 'one of the greatest buildings in the world'.

Houses in the shadow of the Majestic Liverpool Cathedral.

Johnny's home was also not too far from the River Mersey and the port where his dad worked as a dock labourer. It was an insecure and irregular cattle-market-style, casual labour system, and he was earning a paltry weekly wage that provided minimal food, rent and clothing for the large impoverished family, who were literally living on the breadline.

The docks and its bustling surroundings again provided a great play area for the local children, who would hang on the back of lorries driving in and out of the busy port.

The Toxteth area was a diverse, multicultural melting pot, with a mixed community of White, Chinese and African families all living in close proximity. There was a significant Irish immigrant population in the area. Johnny's family were also of Irish descent.

The area sloped down towards the River Mersey and had a great friendly community spirit, with everyone looking out for each other.

In 1937 George Orwell wrote *The Road to Wigan Pier*, which illustrated the extreme poverty and deprivation in northern cities during the 1930s. It was graphic, and the Dickensian level of depression and poverty it revealed—which was rife throughout the area—shocked the whole country. It detailed the bleak, insufferable living conditions the working-class people of the north had to endure, barely surviving on meagre daily rations and living in cold, damp dwellings. Liverpool was one of the many northern cities George Orwell visited for his research, and he was appalled by the degree of poverty and hardship the working-class people had to tolerate. However, he also noted, surprisingly, that the people had a defiant, steadfast, humorous spirit.

Mass unemployment, poverty and hunger was commonplace in the midst of The Great Depression—which originated in the US economic crash of 1929 and spread east rapidly—and a worldwide economic slump .

The horrors and poverty of the economic depression were compounded by the rapid rise of fascism as Hitler and the Nazis rose to power in Germany. This fanatical extremism was similarly followed a few years later when Franco unleashed four years of murderous civil war in Spain.

Kids living in impoverished conditions

It was against this background of depression, hunger and mass unemployment, together with widespread political unrest, that young Johnny grew up.

Johnny was a short, stocky, strong, tough young boy whose twin sister, Elizabeth, had tragically died of severe consumption—commonplace in poor working-class families at that time—at only a year old.

Growing up on the tough streets of the south end of Liverpool since his birth in 1916 had made him streetwise and more than capable of looking after himself against anybody who fancied their chances with him or his brothers. He never looked for trouble, but when it came he was always ready and willing to face it head on with his combative manner and boxing talent.

He loved reading books from the local library and was very numerate, which was unusual in those poverty-stricken times of poor education and general lack of learning facilities.

Johnny was a warm-hearted, likeable and well-mannered young boy ... until he was provoked, of course; then he would change instantly into a fighting street warrior of some note. He was always prepared to stand his ground, regardless of the size or reputation of his aggressor.

He caught the eye of a school sports teacher, who encouraged him to join the local boxing club, where he stood out as a serious prospect. This kept him away from the rife gang culture in the area.

He was as hard as nails, with a vicious knockout punch, which he became known for in the Toxteth area.

This was typified one fine summer's day in 1932. He had left school a few years earlier and was now approaching 16 years of age. He and his brothers went to see a travelling fairground in nearby Sefton Park, Aigburth. This was a popular annual event with all the local families, as it was a cheap day out for them all, with lots to do and see. The park was a large, grand Victorian landscaped leisure venue of mature trees, extensive flowers, bushes and a large picturesque lake at the centre filled with many ducks and swans. The large park was surrounded by stylish and well-to-do private properties. It was a great place for family picnics, with children playing and peacefully enjoying the warm summer weather.

They were all intrigued to see a boxing ring set up at the fairground, with a large sign saying 'All Comers Welcome'!

A man with a large moustache, a fancy suit and a top hat was inviting—through a loudhailer—anybody brave enough to take on the big bruiser in the ring to win some substantial prize money. If anybody could go three rounds—each three minutes long—with this tough-looking brute, they would win the princely sum of £5! This was a substantial sum in the depressive, impoverished days of 1932.

As they approached the surrounding crowd, one poor battered-and-bruised chap was being carried out of the ring, sadly looking the worse for wear.

The brothers urged Johnny to get up and have a go against the fearsome monster in the ring.

Johnny was initially reluctant, but he thought about what the money would buy for the family. It would greatly help his beloved mother stock up on some much-needed food and other general household basics.

The man in the ring bellowed enthusiastically for someone to take the challenge, and the crowd looked nervously around for another foolhardy volunteer to step forward.

After a bit more persuasion from his brothers, Johnny put his hand up and calmly climbed up the steps into the ring.

The brute looked even bigger and meaner close up, but Johnny was relaxed and quietly confident as his opponent glared at him threateningly across the ring.

The crowd all cheered excitedly for their local boy as the bell sounded loudly for the first round.

The bruiser—being an old-school, experienced veteran boxer—held Johnny and prevented him from throwing a punch. He used his head and other unfair grappling means to prevent Johnny from getting his usual powerful punches in.

This frustrated Johnny for the whole of the first round, as he was not able to launch any of his famous hooks because of all the negative stalling and holding tactics from his old, seasoned opponent, who had done this many times before and fully knew the drill.

But the crowd and his brothers cheered and shouted his name at every swing, which encouraged him and gave him more confidence.

The first round ended on the bell with just about honours even and the crowd clapping and cheering wildly for their local boy.

The second-round bell went, and Johnny strode confidently into the centre of the ring. In a blinding flash, he landed a short right hook solidly onto the bruiser's chin, decking him instantly into a bewildered daze, floundering onto the canvas floor. He was counted out and a bucket of water thrown over him to arouse his crumpled body from the dusty, blood-stained canvas.

The manager looked shocked as the crowd cheered and shouted wildly with delight. Johnny just smiled at his brothers and said nothing while his winning arm was held high in the air.

When the ringmaster gave him the prize money, he asked Johnny if he would like the job in the ring permanently for a weekly wage, albeit a fairly modest one. Johnny accepted without hesitation, as money was scarce in those days and it would help the family coffers tremendously.

He told his mum and dad, and although a little concerned about his welfare and safety, they were delighted with the new unexpected source of family income.

Johnny joined the travelling fair for several months, doing well and enjoying the many bouts—most easy and some quite tough—which kept him in good physical shape and extremely fit.

Eventually, he got bored and homesick, greatly missing his family, so he decided to return home to Liverpool and the family home in Toxteth to reunite with his loved ones.

They were all delighted to see him again, especially his beloved mum, albeit that she would miss the regular, much-needed extra income, which had been a real godsend for her.

Johnny now seriously considered his future and looked for a suitable job to help support his parents.

CHAPTER TWO

ARMY ENLISTMENT

Johnny tried many different jobs after leaving school with no academic qualifications and a very basic education. In general, they were an assortment of manual labouring jobs, which he enjoyed, as it kept his physique in great shape and he had loved any form of manual work since he was a kid.

He worked on a variety of building sites for the gas board and other employers, earning much-needed money for his family. His toughest job was probably being a 'flagger', which required tremendous physical effort and strength. It required picking up heavy rectangular concrete slabs by hand and laying them side by side. He did this eight hours a day on various building sites and housing projects.

His frame and physique filled out rapidly into a solid, muscular shape, and he kept up his amateur boxing and training at the local club.

In 1939, when he had just turned 23, there was a countrywide recruitment drive by the army because of all the military and political unrest brewing on the mainland of Europe. After some thought and a lengthy discussion with his parents, brothers and friends, Johnny decided to give it a go and join up. He was assigned to the Royal Artillery 3rd HAA.

He of course enjoyed the hard physical training and exercise and also took up the opportunity to volunteer for the army boxing team, where he naturally excelled and greatly impressed all the staff. He was so impressive in the trials that his selection for the army team was inevitable, and he soon established himself as a feared opponent throughout the ranks.

His military reputation grew rapidly as, with his superb boxing skills and ever-improving knockout punch prowess, he won many army boxing tournaments and trophies. His superior officers were delighted with his disciplined attitude and progress, and he was soon promoted to the rank of bombardier.

In the dark days of 1940 Germany had already invaded Norway and the long-expected invasion of France and the Low Countries was well underway. As resistance by the French and Belgian armies had somewhat surprisingly and unfortunately collapsed, the British Expeditionary Force withdrew to the French coast at Dunkirk, where it was eventually evacuated in early June.

The new prime minister, Winston Churchill, was far from happy and issued a notice to all the chiefs of staff: 'The completely defensive habit of mind, which has ruined the French, must not be allowed to ruin our own initiative. It is of the highest consequence to keep the largest numbers of German forces all along the coasts of the countries that have been conquered, and we should immediately set to work to organise raiding forces on these coasts where the populations are still friendly to us. Such forces may be composed of self-contained, thoroughly equipped units of say 1,000 up to not less than 10,000 men when combined.' Two days later he elaborated: 'Enterprises must be prepared of specially trained troops of the hunter class, who can develop a reign of terror first of all on the "butcher and bolt" policy. I look to the chiefs of staff to propose me measures for a vigorous, enterprising and ceaseless offensive against the whole German occupied coastline.'

Although Churchill was a key supporter and both adamant and passionate about this new concept of guerrilla warfare, there was a reluctance from some in the military high command who were not as enthusiastic about the idea. Other generals found the idea to be wasteful and considered Special Forces to be unnecessary, costly 'private armies'.

The first recruits were volunteers selected from existing army regiments throughout Great Britain. Later, in 1942, the Royal Navy's Royal Marine battalions were also reorganised as commandos. The name 'commando' was used for these special troops; it was borrowed from the guerrilla fighters of The Boer War by Lt Colonel Dudley Clarke, who said:

The objective of forming a commando unit is to collect together a force of individuals trained to fight independently as an irregular and not as a formed military unit. The procedure for raising and maintaining commandos is as follows. One or two leaders in each command will be selected as commando leaders. They will each be ordered to select from their own command a number of troop leaders to serve under them. The troop leaders will in turn select the officers and men to form their own troop.

While no strengths have yet been decided upon, I have in mind commandos of a strength of something like ten troops of fifty men in each. Each troop will have a commander and one or possibly two other officers.

After the successful evacuation of Dunkirk, Prime Minister Winston Churchill sanctioned and authorised the new crack fighting force of specially selected soldiers to be expertly trained and formed into what would eventually develop into today's elite force known as the SAS.

They were looking for the toughest and roughest candidates from all over the UK. They needed to be fearless in order to form spasmodic, strategic attacks on the enemy. They would operate a special operations unit to wreak havoc, with all-out devastating raids from behind the enemy lines. The concept was to use this new combat force to attack the enemy with quick, well-planned raids with frightening precision, wreaking a constant reign of terror on the alarmed and unsuspecting Germans.

The new commando unit was expertly trained at secret locations in Scotland. They were trained in physical fitness, survival, orienteering, close-quarter combat, silent killing, signalling, amphibious and cliff assault, vehicle operation, multi-weapon handling and, last but not least, punitive demolition skills. Any man who failed to live up to the stringent requirements of the training schedule would be 'returned to unit' immediately.

Johnny's reputation as being a tough, no-nonsense fighter and hard man proved him to have the perfect credentials for the new project, and he was highly recommended for the combat regiment was and sent by train to the secret training camp at Scapa Flow, Scotland.

Only the toughest and most fearless soldiers—some of whom were unorthodox, rebellious types—were gathered together in the north of Scotland to train in new unique close-combat methods that had never been used before in the military. These men were hand-picked for their fearless characters and hard-nosed personalities, and in many cases they were real rogues and tearaways who disliked too much formality and unnecessary army discipline. The infamous and legendary 'Paddy' Mayne, DSO (Distinguished Service Order) and three Bars, was a prime example of the tough cavalier characters selected for the new fighting force. Mayne was an intelligent man— in fact, he was a lawyer—and he was also a great rugby player and had represented both Ireland and the British Lions. He had a fierce reputation as an aggressive fighter and was also, like Johnny, a prolific amateur boxer. His exploits for brawling and getting into trouble with his superiors because of his unorthodox and sometimes rebellious manner became infamous throughout the ranks. He was allegedly under arrest for striking an officer when he was invited by David Stirling, the commanding officer of the new unit, to join the new 'butcher and bolt' raiding force. He fitted the bill perfectly as a proper no-nonsense tough guy, always ready for a fight. He was a fearless warrior who eventually rose through the ranks to lieutenant colonel, becoming one of the most honoured and decorated officers in the British Army. He was also in the Royal Artillery coming from County Down and went on to become one of the most legendary figures in the subsequent North African raids that wrought havoc on the enemy in that warfare region. He even received the Croix de Guerre, France's highest honour! Even more controversially, he was denied the Victoria Cross, although it was actually authorised and approved by Montgomery himself.

Paddy and Johnny were the exact fit for this new unit and its planned structure. Once they were in action and unleashed, their bravery and courage would wreak terror through the enemy, with maximum impact.

The training was intense, physical and tough, with emphasis on unorthodox combat methods that would be lethal, unexpected by the enemy and carried out with carefully planned precision. The attacks by fierce commando raiding parties had only one mission: to go in swiftly and create as much destruction behind the lines as possible, and just as quickly to get out.

They were trained in demolition, weapons and navigation. The training was intense and arduous, with a great emphasis on fitness, combat and survival, which in Johnny's case would prove fortuitously useful in the horrific times ahead that he was destined to experience. The typical daily training routine was reveille at 6 am, a mile training run at 7 am, followed by PT exercises and then breakfast at 8 am. They would then be on parade for inspection at 9 am. The morning was completed with a long route march of about 8 to 10 miles in full arms and battle dress at a very fast pace; this included cross-country, map-reading, compass-reading and moving silently through cover. Lunch was at 1 pm, followed by a swimming parade of ninety minutes of fast lengths, then fast running and more physical exercising. Tea was at 4.30 pm, followed by a forty-five-minute lecture at 5 pm. After 6 pm, the evening was free for personal time and other company duties.

On one particular day, at a training session, the group were being shown the safe way to handle a hand grenade and the importance of throwing it as soon as the pin is released and it becomes active and ready to explode. The instructor released the pin and appeared to accidentally drop the live grenade on the floor right in front of all the men in the group. Everybody in Johnny's unit scattered in a mad, frantic panic, but Johnny didn't flinch and stood his ground, eye to eye with the instructing officer. He stood there calmly, staring at the officer, who stared back at him! The officer asked him why he had not run away like the others, and Johnny replied that neither had the officer, so it must have been a dud to purposely test the group!

Although tough and fearless, Johnny had a softer side, and a typical Scouse sense of humour too, always happy to hear or share a joke and always ready and willing to help his fellow soldiers whenever they needed assistance or advice.

Captain David Stirling, Paddy Mayne, Johnny and the rest of the selected units of men and officers were all founding members of this fearless fighting institution. Little did Johnny know that the combat training he received would prove very useful in the trying times that lay ahead for him.

CHAPTER THREE

RETURNED TO UNIT

After about nine months of intensely tough combat training, Johnny completed his training programme and became a fully fledged member of this new crack combat battalion. Their sole purpose was to reinforce Churchill's master plan to wreak havoc on the enemy at a moment's notice and instil fear and shock throughout their ranks. They were trained to cause as much damage and carnage as possible in their carefully planned, daring raids behind enemy lines.

At a celebration evening held in the mess, Johnny was enjoying a pint of the beer with a few of his friends, winding down and having a good chinwag and a few laughs. A couple of Scottish officers were standing next to the group and told them in an abrupt, aggressive manner to keep the noise down. One of the group objected, but Johnny told him to take no notice and just ignore them. One of the officers made a mocking remark about his short stature and why he had been selected for the unit, using a derogatory slang term. The officers were two burly built Scots, and they continued to goad the group with more insulting remarks.

This verbal barrage, unfortunately for them, lit the proverbial blue touchpaper for Johnny, who reacted swiftly and instantly. A flashing short right hook exploded, and one of the officers hit the floor dramatically, dropping his drink, which smashed in pieces all over the mess floor. The other officer then took a swing, missed and felt the full force of another sucker punch, which left him sprawled out on the mess floor too. Both officers lay prostrate on the mess floor, much to the amusement of Johnny's group, who cheered and slapped him on the back in support.

The next morning Johnny was ordered to attend the commanding officer's office to 'face the music' for the previous night's controversial incident. The commanding officer put him at ease and asked for a full and detailed explanation for his actions.

After hearing what Johnny had to say, he sympathised with him but ordered him to apologise to the two officers formally. Once the apology was made, he explained, the matter would then be officially finished and they could all move on with more important matters.

But Johnny was absolutely adamant that he would not apologise, as he believed he was not in the wrong and the two officers had got what they deserved. He felt strongly that the two 'jocks' were totally out of order for their derogatory comments, aggressive behaviour and verbal insults towards him and the other men.

The commanding officer smiled and said that he fully understood and was, in fact, most understanding and sympathetic to Johnny's reaction, but he insisted the apology was necessary, emphasising that it was purely a regulatory requirement and formality.

Johnny, however, was stubborn and steadfast, and determined to stick firmly to his position. He once again blatantly refused—in a firm, polite and courteous manner—to apologise.

The commanding officer explained that unless he apologised formally, he would have no alternative but to RTU (Returned to Unit) him immediately. However, he also said that given his impeccable training record and his proven fighting ability he did not want to lose him from the newly formed crack combat unit.

Johnny thanked the commanding officer again, politely, and said that he fully understood his position but would not be apologising to anybody for his actions, no matter what the resulting consequences would be.

The commanding officer shook his head in mounting frustration, disbelief and sheer disappointment but asked him firmly, for the last and final time, would it be a formal apology or a RTU order?

Johnny instantly replied, stubbornly and without any hesitation, 'RTU, sir.' He packed his personal things said goodbye to his unit and headed to the station for a long, thoughtful train ride back to his old unit in the Royal Artillery.

Fate was kinder to him than he realised at the time, as many of his unit and close friends lost their lives in a later initial unsuccessful foray into North Africa, which he would have most certainly been a part of had he apologised and avoided the RTU order.

He was sad to leave the newly formed special combat force and all his new friends but perfectly content and satisfied that he had made the right decision.

The intense combat training schedule he had now completed was important, but not as important to him as the survival techniques and ability to endure captivity and torture, should it ever happen to him. But at the time he was totally oblivious how this training would help him eventually help him survive the frightening hell and horrors that lay ahead waiting for him. He was in for some difficult times in the years to come as World War Two began to escalate and spread rapidly throughout the globe.

CHAPTER FOUR

SHIPPED TO SINGAPORE

Johnny had settled back into the day-to-day military routine of his old unit at the Royal Artillery when they suddenly received orders to ship out to Singapore in the Far East. This was in support of the troubling Far Eastern conflict with Japan. This news came as a great surprise to him, and indeed the whole barracks.

The troop carrier vessel was massive and set off to Singapore via a stopover for refuelling and restocking supplies in South Africa.

The trip was relatively relaxed, except for the exhausting daily training and physical tests—much to Johnny's delight, as he loved keeping himself ultra fit doing the rigorous training exercises.

On arrival in Singapore, the fourth largest port in the world, the tropical heat was intense and the humidity even more uncomfortable, but gradually it became just about bearable as they settled into their new quarters and daily military routine.

Singapore is an island at the southern end of the Malay Peninsula, sandwiched between Malaysia and Indonesia in South East Asia. It was considered a vital part of the British Empire, being supposedly impregnable as a fortress. It was known as 'the Gibraltar of the East'.

Johnny was an integral part of the Royal Artillery 29th HAA Battery on the heavy ack-ack guns, which required a great deal of physical power, discipline and concentration. These were his main strengths as a fully trained combat soldier.

The guns were all pointed out towards the sea from Singapore, as the High Command military experts had thought that any offensive enemy would attack from the sea, not from the rear. The area behind them was a vast area of wild, dense tropical jungle infested with thick mangrove swamps that theoretically, and somewhat ironically, was supposed to protect them from any possible enemy attack. The huge gun placements would, of course, be ineffective against any 'unlikely' enemy attacks from the rear because of the logistical difficulty of repositioning them into new placements.

The jungle was dark, dense and almost impenetrable. It was impossible to even contemplate an army coming through such a thick, tangled and formidable natural barrier.

This is why the Allied High Command were confident that any Japanese attack would only come from the sea, which was sufficiently protected by the forward-pointing heavy artillery.

Depending on the defensive nature of the jungle was a grave mistake by the British-led forces and left them totally exposed and outmanoeuvred when the conflict finally and alarmingly commenced. Little did the Allied forces realise that this was exactly what the Japanese forces had been planning to do.

This strategy gave them a distinct advantage, as the heavy artillery was virtually impossible to reposition at such short notice. Also, Singapore's huge fortifications and gun placements were fairly old, even though the military base had been upgraded in 1938.

This oversight was a classic example of the naivety, arrogance and inadequate planning by Britain in the face of the Japanese aggression towards the West in numerous key locations.

This Japanese attack on Singapore happened at almost the same time as their shocking surprise attack on the American naval base in Pearl Harbour, Hawaii, which destroyed half the American battle fleet.

Also, the RAF had virtually lost all its frontline fighter planes after the Japanese had attacked the airfields in Singapore and destroyed them all with a destructive bombardment, so any hope of the much-needed RAF aerial support for the Allied forces was dashed before the attack on Singapore had even actually begun.

However, Britain's naval presence in Singapore at that time had been strengthened by a small number of warships stationed there, led by the ultra-modern battleship the HMS *Prince of Wales* and the much more ageing battle cruiser the HMS *Repulse*.

But disaster struck the Allies once again, when after heading out to sea northwards up the Malay Peninsula coast with no available air cover, they were both attacked and sunk by repeated sustained attacks from Japanese torpedo bombers, again with no protection from the RAF fighter planes.

The loss of both ships had a devastating effect on the Allied forces' morale.

Now only the Army was left to counter and possibly stop the inevitable Japanese attack on Singapore.

While the Japanese forces were all battle-hardened, experienced troops, with a cult-like determination and frenzied passion to destroy their enemies, the Allied forces was a melting pot of several inexperienced international nations—consisting of troops from Britain, Australia, Malaya, Burma and India—who fought under leaders who were divided by languages, ideology and political allegiance. Also, the British force in particular was more suited to— and armed and equipped for—a traditional campaign in Western Europe or the Western Desert, certainly not for equatorial jungle warfare and the difficult logistics of the area, which affected supplies and movement adversely due to the difficult and varied terrain.

Finally, the unexpected surprise Japanese attack from the rear suddenly a few weeks after their arrival—and the subsequent fighting—was intense, rampaging and fierce. Non-stop air raids at will and a constant bombardment of heavy artillery rained down on the Allies and continuously pounded the Singapore docks, the whole city infrastructure and the surrounding areas.

The Japanese bombardment and attacks were relentless, and the Allied troops were pinned back and retreated each day, while rapidly running out of supplies and ammunition.

This was mainly due to the naive underestimation of the threat from the Japanese and their troops' battle-hardened military capabilities. The Japanese skilfully deployed tanks, which the British had thought impractical for use within the dense jungle terrain. Their infantry troops even used old bicycles to aid their rapid advance. The scale of these fast attacks never allowed the thinly spread British troops to re-group from the rampaging relentless assault.

It was so ironic, this Japanese attack from the rear, as this was exactly what Johnny had been expertly trained for with the special forces unit in Scotland before he was returned to unit for his refusal to apologise.

Although it was a relatively short two-week battle, many thousands were killed, and even many more were severely wounded and badly maimed.

The Imperial Japanese Army was, of course, well versed in warfare strategy and were experienced fighters, having been at war with China since 1937.

The British troops and Allies, although greater in number, were spread relatively thinly over a large area and were wide open to be outflanked and overrun by the marauding enemy through there thin, scattered line.

The Japanese onslaught was rapid and seemingly unstoppable, and they had been given a specific mandate to kill, destroy and not take any prisoners during battle.

This ferocious barrage took the Allied forces by surprise as it advanced at such a swift and remarkable pace.

Against all the usual rules of war and agreed convention guidelines, they were ordered to execute all in their path, with absolutely no mercy, and they swept into Singapore like a veritable tsunami, leaving death, devastation and destruction in their wake. Without having to stop, restrain and corral any prisoners, they were able to move swiftly over the ground and rapidly advance on Singapore itself.

Wounded soldiers were savagely killed where they lay, and those who surrendered were ruthlessly murdered on the spot. Some captured prisoners were even doused with petrol and burnt to death in the many frenzied attacks.

One of the horrendous early examples of Japanese barbarity was witnessed at the Alexandra Barracks Hospital. As the Japanese broke through and advanced towards the hospital, a British lieutenant approached them as an envoy, carrying a white flag of truce.

He was bayonetted to death on the spot. The Japanese troops then entered the hospital and killed fifty Allied soldiers, including some who were undergoing surgery at the time. Many doctors and nurses were also killed savagely in cold blood where they stood.

The next day the remaining 200 staff and patients, who had been assembled and tied up the previous day, many walking wounded, were ordered to march 400 yards to an industrial area. Those who fell down on the way were bayonetted to death, and the rest were forced into a series of small, cramped, badly ventilated rooms. They were held overnight without water or food. Some died as a result of this wicked treatment.

The next morning the remainder were all callously and ruthlessly bayonetted to death.

The sadistic and savage Massacre of Alexandra Barracks Hospital was a frightening indication of what was to come in the years ahead.

This atrocity was typical of the inhumane behaviour of the Japanese troops towards all their enemies. whether military or civilian.

The British troops fell back to the island of Singapore, destroying the causeway and prepared for a long siege. Unfortunately, the famed heavy coastal-pointing guns were mostly armed with armour-piercing shells designed to pierce the hulls of warships, but were virtually ineffective against infantry targets. High-explosive shells would have given the Japanese a much bigger problem and caused a lot more enemy infantry losses, which would have balanced the odds more favourably.

BL 15-inch coastal defense gun elevated for firing,
Singapore, circa 1941

After two weeks of heavy bombing, air strikes and even hand-to-hand combat, the Allied forces High Command decided that now the only option—given the lack of resources, damaged water supply, limited artillery, lack of air cover and little or no support from their own High Command back home—was to negotiate a surrender. This was agreed and formally finalised on 15 February 1942.

Ironically, the Japanese themselves were also struggling with limited supplies at that time. However, when Japanese General Yamashita tried a bluff and demanded a full unconditional surrender the Allied High Command 'blinked first' and capitulated under the order of British officer Lieutenant General Arthur Percival, feeling that the British position was now severely untenable. Percival ironically agreed to surrender in an honest but futile effort to try to prevent any further loss of life.

An estimated 100,000 people were taken prisoner in Singapore, of which 9,000 went on to die helping to build the infamous 'Death Railway'.

The remainder—somewhere between 5,000, according to the Japanese, and 50,000, according to the Chinese—perished under the Japanese control of Singapore.

This plan, inspired by the Kempeitai (Japanese Military Police), was an ethnic-cleansing process, referred to as 'Sook Ching', to viscously exterminate all local Chinese deemed to be anti-Japanese. These defenceless Chinese were ruthlessly rounded up and taken to various locations, where they were killed systematically by machine guns and rifles.

This massacre was orchestrated by the Kempeitai, who used local informers to expose any anti-Japanese supporters for immediate execution.

On the Allied side 5,000 were killed during the battle, and a staggering 80,000 more were maimed, badly wounded or captured.

During the fighting and immediately afterwards, many civilians were murdered, allied soldiers were decapitated, prisoners were burnt alive and hospital patients were slaughtered where they lay. This was followed by a ritual massacre of the local Chinese population.

This savagery was a massive shock to the British troops, the majority of whom had never seen any military action until this battle.

Nearly 2,000 Japanese troops were killed and 3,500 wounded in one of the fiercest and most violent battles of World War Two.

Japanese propaganda banners, posters and Rising Sun flags were soon displayed all over Singapore on all major buildings.

The defeat in Singapore was basically due to inadequate planning, minimal jungle training, poor intelligence, low morale, confused command structure and a lack of air cover, together with the blatant underestimation of a battle-hardened enemy.

Johnny was now a captive Japanese prisoner of war, and little did he know of the many horrors and inhumane atrocities that lay ahead for him and his unsuspecting captured comrades. They were in for a truly awful time at the hands of the merciless Japanese troops.

The Japanese treated the Allied prisoners violently, as they felt that by surrendering they had forfeited any due respect and had basically dishonoured themselves. They believed that the prisoners should be treated with no respect or status whatsoever, due to their cowardly and dishonourable surrender. Their own so-called noble code of conduct regarded

surrender as shameful. This was a code inspired by the ideology of Japan's ruling warlord elite and underwritten by a strong state religion and cult-like emperor worship. This demanded lemming-like levels of self-sacrifice and obedience from their submissive and frenzied troops, with no parallel anywhere else in the civilised world at that time.

These spurious and clearly hypocritical 'principles' were incredibly ironic, given their own eventual complete and total unconditional surrender to the Allied forces many years later.

CHAPTER FIVE

THE SURRENDER

The Japanese army marched victoriously through the centre of Singapore and accepted the official formal unconditional surrender of the Allied forces from Lieutenant-General Arthur Percival. Johnny was bitterly dismayed at the order, as his own innate instinct was always to fight to the end, no matter what, and never give in. But he was now sadly resigned to his fate.

The Japanese soldiers were particularly cruel and vindictive, treating the prisoners of war with total and utter contempt and complete disrespect and brutality. They took every opportunity, evidently with great pleasure, to inflict severe physical violence when given the slightest excuse to do so—a slap, punch, dig or a quick blow with a rifle butt or stinging bamboo cane. The painful butt of a rifle in the ribs or a vicious unexpected backhand slap in the face was hard for Johnny to take; however, his strong willpower and powerful mentality, plus his intense combat training, enabled him to count to ten and tolerate the constant physical abuse and provocation from his captors.

His special forces training helped him restrain his retaliatory instincts towards the Japanese, who obviously enjoyed the constant and deliberate provocation of their defenceless and weary prisoners.

Johnny and his battalion were marched in the searing tropical heat through the streets, in front of the astonished locals, to the infamous Changi Prison to await their unimaginable fate. Changi was known for its horrendous conditions and minimal daily rations, and many men died from malnutrition, disease, harsh physical treatment and constant torture and punishment.

Johnny was fiercely determined to survive the ordeal, and his strong and focused willpower was his greatest asset.

Japanese guards escorting Allied troops

Changi was a filthy, unbearable hellhole of a prison, but nothing compared to what was to come for this young 25-year-old boy from the backstreets of Liverpool.

The character, humour and spirit of the prisoners kept everyone going, but the cup of tasteless rice and water they received was insufficient to keep them healthy and fit. This malnourishment led to rapid physical and mental deterioration and resulted in numerous fatalities.

The daily beatings and lack of decent food inevitably wore down the spirit and will of the prisoners, and many of them became weak and ill with diseases such as malaria, beriberi, dysentery and jaundice. Many had pus-filled, septic ulcers gaping open to the white bone, causing them to give up and sadly just fade away.

The heroic medical staff did their best but had little medication and implements to ease the awful suffering of the dying and sick prisoners, who were increasing in numbers by the day.

Marching to the Surrender meeting.

After several months of primitive incarceration in Changi, just about managing to survive, Johnny was informed that he was being transferred to an unknown destination.

This was a bit disconcerting, to say the least, as he pondered what horrors lay ahead for him and his fellow prisoners at the hands of his sadistic Japanese captors.

The Japanese told the officers and men that there would be far better conditions and decent nourishment for them, but it was just a ruse to lull them into a false sense of hope. On many occasions, to persuade and coerce the men to move from camp to camp, the Japanese coaxed them with spurious promises of better conditions at the next stop, along with more food and medical support.

CHAPTER SIX

THE SAIGON DOCKS

In April 1942 Johnny and other selected prisoners were marched from Changi Prison to the dockside at Keppel Harbour under the direct command of Lieutenant Colonel Hugonin. They were literally crammed onto to a hot sweaty cargo ship named the *Nissyo Maru*.

They were forced into a dark, cramped and unventilated hold, which was filthy, musty and stifling, and uncomfortable for the already-undernourished, sick, weary prisoners. It was difficult to breathe in the overcrowded and confined conditions, and the constant moaning and painful cries and pleas from the prisoners was heart-wrenching.

The filthy conditions and minimal rations, consisting of a meagre portion of rice and the odd cup of water, caused a surge in severe dysentery among the prisoners, and the six-day journey by sea was a gut-wrenching ordeal for all of them, with little rest or sleep.

Finally, after more than a week of this uncomfortable journey, Johnny and his fellow prisoners arrived at their next destination in Saigon (Ho Chi Minh City), Indochina. From then on they were referred to as 'the Saigon battalion'.

Saigon was one of the largest and busiest shipping centres in the South China Sea and was the main hub for the Imperial Japanese Army. It was used mainly to send their troops, equipment and supplies in their frantic push northwards towards Thailand and their main destination of Burma via the dreadful infamous Thai-Burma Railway (the Death Railway).

On arrival they were marched forcefully by Japanese guards to the Saigon Docks into what looked like old wooden stables and huts. They were forced to work from dawn till dusk, like slaves, loading and unloading war materials and supplies onto the merchant and military ships. These items were for urgent transmission and onward shipment northwards to support the ever-increasing numbers of rampaging Japanese invading forces.

Johnny's first thought was how he could sabotage the shipments to the detriment of the Japanese, which, to be fair, was the thought of everybody in the ranks, from Colonel Hugonin down. Although everybody was in a poor physical and mental state, they were determined to do anything in their power to deter and adversely affect the progress of the Japanese mighty war effort and rapid advance northwards to Burma.

Johnny started by throwing small items from the crates overboard whenever he had the opportunity and as much critical war equipment and materials as possible. This had to be done discreetly, without being seen by the supervising Japanese guards, who were watchful and alert on board most of the time. He even threw oil barrels, tools and weapons overboard whenever he could, which was extremely dangerous and risky. If he was caught, he would most certainly be tortured and would no doubt face a subsequent swift execution—the Japanese executed prisoners for less-serious misdemeanours, such as stealing basic food or supplies. Any attempted escapees were also certain to receive a fatal punishment after some savage physical torture.

The Saigon Battalion, as they were now known, were in for a truly horrific time of forced slave labour, little nourishment, brutality and barbaric treatment from the Japanese, who would viciously assault a prisoner without reason or provocation, just to assert their superiority over their captors and keep them meekly subservient.

The Japanese guards in Saigon were even more violent than those at Changi Prison, and they made the prisoners' lives a misery with their constant screaming of orders all day long.

The prisoners were housed in filthy, dusty stables infested with flies, bugs, lice and tropical mosquitoes. The majority of them suffered from malaria, dysentery and beriberi—among other debilitating tropical diseases—with virtually no medical supplies and minimal portions of maggoty rice and water to survive on.

Over 1,100 prisoners were sent to Saigon on this forced labour, but numbers sadly decreased rapidly with the inevitable deaths caused by malnutrition and disease.

The prisoners continued to carry out attempts of sabotage. Anything they could do to damage Japanese war materials and equipment was done out at every opportunity by prisoners of every rank, even at the risk of personal punishment.

Johnny removed parts from weapons, drained aviation oil and removed leads and parts from military vehicles, all to cause as many logistical problems for the Japanese as possible. This lifted the spirits of all concerned.

There were two infamous executions in relation to a brave and courageous, but unfortunately failed, escape attempt by men from the battalion. The vicious execution of two escapees, who were caught after a day and a half on the run, caused great horror, sadness and anger in the battalion. Baxter and Cassidy of the Royal Artillery 3rd HAA were callously and savagely executed. This shocked the whole battalion. The Japanese used this as a sinister warning and deterrent to rest of the prisoners. This caused great fury throughout the group, but the Japanese showed no mercy or emotion and seemed to enjoy and mock the prisoners' grief.

Another savage incident occurred when a Japanese guard hit a prisoner hard with his rifle and the man retaliated and forcefully smacked the guard in the face. Other guards jumped in and battered the prisoner viciously to the ground and gave him a really good hiding. Not long later the prisoner died from the effects of the ferocious beating.

Johnny endured fifteen long and tiring months on the Saigon Docks, working from eleven to eighteen hours a day in unbearable tropical heat and energy-sapping conditions, being treated like a slave.

After this lengthy and arduous ordeal he was transferred to Thailand, together with 700 of the so-called 'fittest' prisoners from the Saigon Battalion, for work on the dreaded 'Death Railway'. They were marched to the Saigon Docks and packed tightly onto three old battered riverboats that sailed off on the long journey northwards up the Mekong River. Two tiring days later they arrived at Phnom Penh, Cambodia, and were force-marched to the main railway station.

Packed like animals into closed and stiflingly hot goods wagons, they then had an uncomfortable 400-mile train journey, eventually crossing the Thailand border in the late evening, exhausted.

After a brief stop at Bangkok for some much-needed sustenance, consisting of rice and water, they set off by train to Nong Pla Duk. They remained there for a few days before being force-marched to Ban Pong. They were then packed into railway wagons already filled with sleepers, rails and other supply items, for another most uncomfortable, hot journey to the Tha Sao camp. Here the horrors of life on the infamous Thai-Burma Death Railway soon became a reality for the tired and weary men of the Saigon Battalion.

The next morning they were loaded onto trucks and taken down to the muddy riverbank, where they were unceremoniously packed onto flimsy barges for the dangerous journey upriver to Kinsayok, where the main prisoner-of-war camp was based

Another hot, cramped and uncomfortable journey ensued upriver, and the start of even more nightmares for this young, 'fit' but weary Liverpudlian boy.

Their first task was to build living quarters for themselves before joining the main camp prisoners—who were already established in their cramped, primitive living conditions—on the railway work schedule.

The conditions were even more extreme and far worse than in Saigon. The battalion lost a fifth of its numbers in the first month alone due to disease, malnourishment and the constant torture and abuse from the vicious Japanese and Korean guards.

Lieutenant Colonel Hugonin was a courageous character who constantly appealed to the Japanese on behalf of his men for better treatment. In spite of many slaps, and threats from the Japanese officers that he would be shot if he didn't toe the line, he persisted in demanding more food and other urgent necessary items for the prisoners.

The men respected this brave and principled officer for his stubborn resistance of—and brave confrontations with—the Japanese, even though he was beaten up badly on many occasions. He was truly a courageous and principled leader who always stuck up for his men, regardless of the consequences or punishment to himself.

One particular incident occurred when the Japanese required the prisoners to sign an official document saying they would never attempt to escape from captivity. Hugonin ordered the men not to obey, on the grounds that it was every British soldier's categorical duty to try to escape and get back to their lines at every possible opportunity. The Japanese went mad at this impertinent refusal and savagely beat the colonel up in front of the men, but he still stubbornly and bravely refused. So the Japanese callously stopped all the much-needed food rations as a severe punishment for the camp. The colonel then ordered all the men to sign the document using a made-up name rather than their own: Errol Flynn, Clarke Gable, Mickey Mouse—anything but their own.

The gleeful Japanese were absolutely delighted with this quick, apparently weak, compliance and allowed the food allocation to recommence, thinking that the prisoners had meekly succumbed to their threats.

Hugonin was a fine officer and leader, but more importantly he was a great man who stood up for his fellow officers at the risk of his own safety and survival in the face of harsh and callous treatment. His bravery and defiance in the face of Japanese threats and torture was clear for all the men to see and respect. Seeing him stand up for them against their despised foes, no matter what the consequences were, lifted their spirits greatly during those dark and dismal times.

CHAPTER SEVEN

THE DEATH RAILWAY

On arrival in Kinsayok they were ordered to build a camp in the thick, sweaty, bug-ridden tropical jungle before starting to work on the infamous Thai-Burma Railway. It is said that this railway was built on the thousands of bodies—and the blood and sweat—of captured FEPOW's (Far East Prisoners of War) and the thousands of captive South East Asian labourers (Romusha). They say that there was at least one death for every wooden railway sleeper laid on the Death Railway.

Thailand was technically neutral in the war but had no other option than to cooperate with the more powerful Imperial Japanese Empire and become effectively submissive allies.

In 1942 the Japanese had also seized Burma and taken control from the British, although they had to rely on long, dangerous sea journeys for the transportation of supplies to their troops stationed there. Its proximity to the old British colony of Burma was perfect for a base to prepare for the ongoing offensive against the defending British forces. However, this left them susceptible to sea attacks from the Allies, and a direct rail link was the only other real option.

Unfortunately, the logistics were abysmal for transporting troops, arms and supplies to the battlefield across the Tenasserim Range, which divided Thailand from Burma. Therefore, somehow a new safer and practical overland route was now urgently required for this vital purpose.

The hilly topography, rivers, dense jungle, mangrove swamps, tropical heat and heavy monsoon climate was not conducive to an effective, suitable or practical supply route, and the sea route was too long and was becoming far too dangerous for the Japanese, with the Allied naval superiority in the area.

Conveniently, the informal alliance between Thailand and Japan allowed the Japanese troops full access to the whole Thai infrastructure as required. But perhaps more importantly, they had full use of the abundance of local Asian labour to draw on to assist the thousands of already-captured Allied prisoners.

The Japanese's mind-blowing and inconceivable plan was to construct a new direct railway line. It would be nearly 300 miles long, from Nong Pladuk, Thailand, all the way up to Thanbyuzayat, Burma. The railway would have to be constructed through dense, impenetrable jungle and solid rock, in unbearable stifling tropical heat, to an almost-impossible-to-achieve timescale and urgent schedule.

About 180,000 to 250,000 South East Asian civilians of mixed heritage, known by the Japanese as 'Romusha', were also used as helpers to supplement a workforce of over 60,000 Allied prisoners of war. These innocent workers were also subjected to forced slave labour during the railway's lengthy construction. They laboured constantly under the disciplined and harsh supervision of their Japanese captors, who treated them all with absolute disrespect and total contempt, even more than they did the Allied prisoners of war.

About 90,000 innocent civilians died during that nightmarish time, and more than 15,000 Allied prisoners of war perished in the dreadful and inhumane conditions. They were buried in mass jungle cemeteries and graves, or cremated where the cause of death was the dreaded contagious disease of cholera.

Ironically, a similar railway route had been thoroughly surveyed as a possibility by the British Colonial authorities a lot earlier, in 1885. They rightly declared it to be a virtually impossible and far too dangerous task to even contemplate, never mind attempt to undertake. Therefore, with no interested investment forthcoming, the idea was shelved by the British authorities accordingly.

The Imperial Japanese High Command resurrected the idea but realised it would be a massive undertaking, with initial estimates from their engineers suggesting it would take at least five years to complete, due to the difficult terrain and climate. Needless to say, the Imperial High Command in Tokyo deemed this lengthy timescale totally unacceptable, for obvious reasons, and insisted on a far shorter timescale for completion of this urgent project.

Rather than using their own limited corps of manpower, which in the main was fighting a major battle against the Allied forces, it decided it would put its legions of captured prisoners and Asian labourers to work on the project, with strict Japanese and Korean supervision to ensure a swift and efficient completion.

Work on the railway began in October 1942 and ended in October 1943, which was truly a remarkable feat of engineering by all concerned, but sadly at the great cost of many innocent human lives.

Prisoners at work.

Laying the rails

Incredibly, the railway required 600 bridges to be built, as well as hundreds of viaducts, embankments and cuttings.

Living and working conditions for the remainder of the weary, exhausted men of the battalion were atrocious, as they were existing in abominable squalor and deprivation. The location was considerably worse than even the deplorable, bug-infested quarters they had occupied at the Saigon Docks camp.

The overwork, squalor and tropical diseases quickly took their toll on the men, and because life was unbearable and virtually impossible, many just gave up and died.

Johnny contracted malaria numerous times, beriberi, dysentery and jaundice, but his strong will to survive and his strength of character got him through the most gruesome days.

Even though he was extremely ill, the Japanese still made him join the gruelling work parties every day, no matter what physical shape he was in.

By far the worst and most gruesome of ailments were the pus-filled tropical ulcers on his legs and feet. They actually opened the flesh to the bone and attracted swarms of buzzing blow flies, which laid their eggs on the wounds, resulting in awful maggot infestations.

Many of these deep tropical ulcer lacerations became seriously gangrenous and required urgent amputation. There were, however, limited—and sometimes no—surgical implements to perform the excruciatingly painful life-threatening operations in unhygienic and primitive surroundings, but the medical staff improvised as best they could.

Of the 700 prisoners transferred from the Saigon Docks to the railway, a staggering 140 of them died in the first month. The true human cost, however, was even far greater, as almost a third of the 700-strong Saigon Battalion never came home. Sadly, a great many of those who made it through were blighted by mental trauma and psychological disability for the rest of their lives, haunted by their frightening ordeal.

The Japanese troops treated the men abysmally, like submissive captive slaves, and constantly beat them savagely to keep up the frightening pace of work. The work was non-stop and frenzied, and on just paltry starvation rations lacking any real nourishment or vitamins.

The one Japanese word that none of the prisoners would ever forget—screamed at them ad nauseam—was the dreaded 'Speedo'. This hated word was repeatedly screamed out by the guards and echoed eerily around the camps from dawn till nightfall. When they heard this, the prisoners of war were left in no doubt that they had to work faster and harder or suffer the painful and sometimes fatal consequences.

The Japanese had a strict completion deadline from the Imperial High Command in Tokyo, headed by Emperor Hirohito, and they intended to keep to it at any cost, no matter how many lives were lost. It was so essential for their frantic war effort and supply plans pushing rapidly northwards to the battlefields of Burma.

Twelve thousand Japanese and 800 Koreans were appointed as engineers, supervisors and, of course, guards to oversee the swift construction of the Death Railway project. They were all under strict orders to work every prisoner to their absolute maximum, and to literally work them to death. They were ordered to instil rigid and severe discipline at all times to maximise the output from every single man during each and every daylight hour, without a shred of mercy.

The construction of their basic jungle camp consisted of open-sided barrack huts built with bamboo poles and rough attap thatched roofs, which always leaked onto the men. They were about 60 yards long, with sleeping platforms raised above the ground on either side of a filthy, muddy floor.

The huts were teeming with bugs, lice, tropical insects and the ubiquitous jungle mosquitoes buzzing around the sweaty bodies constantly. About 200 prisoners were packed in to each barracks, giving each man barely a 2-foot-wide space to sleep in. How on earth they survived in these unhealthy, cramped and restricted conditions is beyond belief, but the camaraderie, humour, spirit and sheer willpower got them through this horrendous, relentless adversity forced on them by a cult-like group of bloodthirsty troops.

The Japanese were determined to finish their Death Railway right on schedule, at any cost and no matter how many lives were sacrificed in the frenzied 'Speedo' process, as ordered by their Tokyo masters and their beloved emperor. This 'Speedo' order required the prisoners to work extended hours, with even less food or medical support. In fact, there was an intense 'Speedo' period during the latter part of the construction, when the Japanese became desperate for the completion of the project by a new, even earlier, deadline set by the Tokyo Imperial Command.

Corporal punishment became more severe and more frequent during this period, resulting in an increase in sickness and a higher mortality rate.

The Japanese then requested more prisoners of war from Singapore, and many more British and Australian men were sent to the railway to keep up the punishing 'Speedo' pace, hour by punishing hour.

A wonderfully worded and graphic poem called 'The Speedo Period', written in October 1943 by an Australian prisoner of war named R. H. Kelley, who worked on the railway, summed up the punishing period perfectly.

'Speedo! Speedo! All men work faster',
Shouts the Japanese engineer;
We just carry on at our usual pace,
And make out that we do not hear.
Then in move the guards—Bash! Bash!

Down come rifle butts and bamboo;
The railway's well behind schedule,
Good—that's what we are trying to do.
Death is here all around us,
Along the thick jungle trail;
We've dug cuttings, built embankments and bridges,
And now we are laying the rail.
We work from very early in the morning,
And toil through till noon the next day,
Wearily trudge back to our huts for some food,
Before backspiking the rails that we lay.
This surely can't go on forever,
Somehow, one day it must end;
We'll either make it back to Australia,
Or our belongings taken home by a friend.
But no matter what the outcome,
Rest assured we will have done our share,
To keep the Japanese out of Australia,
So generations can live in peace there.

Such a powerfully worded poem by Mr Kelley, God bless him and his family.

The mammoth project was eventually and unbelievably completed ahead of schedule after more than twelve months, albeit at the unimaginable cost of so many thousands of lives and human misery in the numerous different camps spread along the length of the Death Railway.

The loss of human life was truly heartbreaking and shocking. The British prisoners lost 29 per cent of their numbers, the Australians 31 per cent, the Americans 23 per cent and the Dutch 19 per cent. This was bad enough, but the Romusha Asiatic labourers lost a staggering 90 per cent due to the barbarism and maltreatment.

After the completion of the railway the remainder of the Saigon Battalion were dispersed to other camps in various other regions, including Thailand, Saigon and Japan itself, where several hundred of them were sent.

Some of the battalion sailed from Singapore on another

overcrowded cramped 'hell ship' called the *Kachidoki Maru*. Sadly, the ship was sunk in transit by an American submarine torpedo, and the majority of the battalion were either killed on board, drowned or eaten alive by sharks. Only fifty or so managed to survive the attack. They managed to jump off the ship immediately after the torpedo struck. After a few days drifting in the South China Sea, in freezing conditions, they were picked up by Japanese vessels and taken to Japan.

On arrival they continued their captivity for another twelve months or so, again carrying out various forced labour with the usual minimal nourishment and harsh conditions.

While they were there, they witnessed the mushroom clouds from the two cataclysmic atomic bombs dropped on Hiroshima and Nagasaki.

Once again, fate was good to Johnny, as he was still struggling badly with his malaria and was dropped from the Japan transfer group accordingly, which no doubt saved his life once again.

Instead he was ironically transferred to Tamajao Camp for more work and maintenance duties on the railway, even though he was still very ill and suffering badly. He was only there for about a month when he was urgently sent to Nakom Paton Hospital Camp in a weak state from a recurrence of several serious tropical diseases, including jaundice and his grave recurrent malaria problem.

When the war ended, and as result of these and numerous other atrocities, 111 culpable Japanese officials were tried for war crimes by the Allies, with only thirty-two of them found guilty and executed!

CHAPTER EIGHT

BRIT VS AUSSIE FIGHT

Johnny's reputation as a boxer was well known throughout the camp, and the Australian contingent had a formidable reputable boxing champion of their own too. His name was J. J. Mathews, and it was decided, with permission from the Japanese commanding officer, that he would fight Johnny in a 'Brit vs Aussie' contest for the entertainment of the prisoners, and indeed the inquisitive Japanese guards too.

There was always friendly rivalry, humorous banter and verbal exchanges between the Australians and the British, and this was an opportunity for both sides to enjoy and support their own countryman.

The Australians and the British had always had a fierce sporting rivalry, and it was no different in the prisoner-of-war camps, where the banter was constant; this helped keep up everyone's spirits and friendly braggadocio.

Although both men were in poor physical shape, they still had their boxing skills and pride in their unit, and their country to fight for and defend, as well as the driving vociferous support of their fellow prisoners, which helped urge them on.

The prisoners and guards formed a square in the jungle clearing, and loud, hearty cheers of support were let out as the greatly anticipated fight commenced.

Both men showed their superb boxing talent and fought each other in a fair but competitive manner, neither of them flinching or giving an inch round after round. After ten fairly even rounds of proper technical boxing, with both competitors having cut lips, swollen eyes and facial bruising, the Japanese commanding officer stepped in and stopped the fight, declaring it a draw and saying firmly in pigeon English, 'Very brave men.' He lifted both men's arms to the raucous cheers of the buoyant prisoners.

The whole camp clapped and cheered the two tough combatants in unison, which lifted spirits in the camp that memorable day.

The fight was the talk of the camp, but unknown to Johnny, it was indeed fortuitous and timely—for himself in particular—in a moment of provoked anger a few days later.

As Johnny walked past a guard, who looked at him in a surly, unfriendly manner, the Japanese gave him a vicious, hard slap across the side of his face, catching him painfully on the eye-socket bone.

Johnny, for the first time since his capture, instantly snapped and chinned the surprised guard solidly on the jaw, knocking him flat out cold onto the camp floor with a powerful short but solid right hook.

Three other angry and annoyed Japanese guards jumped in quickly with bayonets pointed at Johnny, about to finish him off on the spot for this unacceptable act of retaliation against one of their own. However, by a stroke of extreme good fortune, the Japanese commanding officer had been watching the incident and loudly shouted his orders for the three irate guards to stand down immediately. He gave this order to stand down presumably because of Johnny's incredible show of bravery, skill and resilience in the fight against the Australian prisoner of war a few days earlier.

The Japanese officer warned Johnny to behave in future, or he would suffer severe consequences, and then allowed him to go back to his daily workload. He was very lucky indeed, as striking a Japanese soldier of any rank was usually the most serious offence, next to escaping, and was usually punishable by torture and summary execution in most camps.

It was surprising that Johnny had lasted so long and tolerated so much punishment before reacting and smacking one of the provocative Japanese guards in retaliation. His special forces combat training had most certainly helped him endure all the previous provocation, but as with the incident with the two Scottish officers, he snapped, but was fortunately once again 'returned to unit' by the surprising mercy of the Japanese commanding officer.

CHAPTER NINE

HARD LABOUR

The work on the railway was not only incredibly difficult in the unbearable tropical heat and bug-infested jungle, but it was also extremely hard manual labour for all the prisoners, seven days a week with little food and no breaks from dawn till dark.

Johnny had a good friend called Reuben Kandler, who was a clerk in the pay corps and not used to rigorous strength-sapping manual labour, and he found the railway work tough and difficult.

They were paired up on the hammer-and-spike duty, which was tough and tiring work and needed more brawn than brain to complete. The spike was a steel metre bar that had to be hammered forcefully into the solid mountainous rock to create a metre-length opening into which the TNT explosive charge was placed before it was detonated by the Japanese, causing an ear-piercing, earth-shattering blowback blast of the rocky area. These metre bars were hammered non-stop into the rock by the weary prisoners at equal intervals, from early morning till the end of the long, tiring day. The Japanese would quickly and carefully put the explosive charge in as soon as the prisoners had finished the hole, not giving them much time to run away for protection, as it exploded almost immediately after insertion.

The massive blowback explosion would bring down thousands of sharp rock fragments, raining directly on top of them, with only their small hoe-like *chungkols* held above their heads for protection. The prisoners of war and the support working party would then carry out the mammoth task of clearing the extensive rubble, in preparation for the next metre hole in the rock to be made.

The hole in the rock had to be completed quickly; the dust and residue from the spike had to be continuously cleared from the bottom of it in order to carry on the hammering, otherwise the hole would block with the congealed dust and the spike would not go down any further. The Japanese would go crazy and smack the men with bamboo canes and rifle butts in a fit of angry frustration if they didn't complete the metre holes in the specific timescale.

Johnny used a clam cork on a bit of wire to scoop the dust and rock fragments out before the next hammering attempt; he had remembered from his building-site and flagging jobs. Most of the other men would alternate between the hammer and spike to give each other a much-needed rest. However, Reuben found it difficult to constantly swing the heavy hammer to make direct and accurate contact with the spike, and sometimes he would hit Johnny's arms by accident in his numerous inaccurate attempts.

Johnny, who had been a labourer and worked as a flagger in Liverpool as a young man and enjoyed manual work, decided to let Reuben just hold the spike while he did all the hammering, which suited them both. This arrangement also protected Johnny's bruised limbs from Reuben's wayward swings.

Reuben was a qualified accountant and bravely and courageously kept a comprehensive record of all the prisoners' personal and military details, which he incredibly kept hidden from the Japanese guards until his eventual release from captivity in 1945. This was an unbelievable act of courage and bravery, and he went to such great extremes to conceal his work. His remarkable feat has greatly helped the survivors and their families, providing them with detailed records of their relatives who were in Japanese captivity. Johnny was, in fact, one of the many prisoners on 'The Prisoner List' that Reuben secretly compiled. These records have since become the subject of a best-selling book of the same name, *The Prisoner List* by Richard Kandler, detailing the incredible brave lengths Reuben went to in order to compile his critically important documents and detailing how he kept them away from the prying eyes of his Japanese captors until his liberation. This was a daring and courageous act on his part, because he knew that if his records were ever discovered, he would certainly have been severely tortured and then swiftly summarily executed. However, in spite of the great personal risk to himself, he still completed his clandestine task. Even though on several occasions he came perilously close to being found out by the Japanese guards and their vigilant military police, the Kempeitai, Reuben completed his mammoth task.

Reuben was a skilled mathematician and taught Johnny many clever and amusing tricks with numbers. These tricks helped pass the time in the huts and kept everyone amused, interested and entertained, which of course helped raise the spirits of the group during these awful times.

Johnny never forgot his old friend Reuben and thankfully became reacquainted with him many years after the war at several FEPOW reunions in London, of which Reuben was an integral senior organising member, having proudly received his well-deserved MBE.

They exchanged stories and memories of their awful prisoner-of war ordeal together with other surviving fellow prisoners, recollecting many incidents and atrocities during captivity.

The South East Asian Romusha labourers (Malay, Tamil, Javanese, Indonesian, Chinese, etc.) suffered a far worse fate than the Allied prisoners during the hammer-and-spike blowback explosions. The Japanese would deliberately detonate the charges while the Romusha were still working in the vicinity of the intended explosion, which would crush and kill many of them under the substantial mountain landslides and heavy falling rubble.

The next working party would clear the area of the residual rubble and fragments, along with the dead bodies of the stricken Romusha tragically caught among it.

The Japanese considered them the to be the lowest of the low, sub-human and, sadly, completely and utterly dispensable.

The filthy and unhygienic conditions they lived in were inhumane, and it is beggar's belief that any of them survived, with the lack of nourishment and medication, together with the constant beatings and torture by the bloodthirsty Japanese guards.

It was pure willpower, spirit and mental strength that enabled Johnny and his comrades to survive the living hell that had befallen them at the hands of this marauding force of military savages.

It is hard to imagine how the subdued and exhausted men could work ten to eleven hours a day in those incredibly harsh conditions. They were used as slave labour and received bullying brutality and relentless aggressive Japanese discipline and incessant torment and provocation, all with little or even no food or water in the sweltering tropical heat.

Most of the prisoners wore nothing but a small loincloth called a 'Jap Happy'. Their bare feet were septically blistered from sharp bamboo thorns and rocks strewn around the jungle floor, and they suffered from diseases like malaria, beriberi, dysentery, jaundice, as well as absolute physical and mental exhaustion from the nightmarish ordeal. The fact that the Japanese could justify using sick and dying men in such a callous way tells you a lot about the character, mentality and attitude of the guards and their Imperial High Command.

They were never even the slightest bit sympathetic and refused to show any mercy whatsoever to the dying and exhausted prisoners under their command and captivity. The harsh continuous cries of 'Speedo, speedo' would ring hauntingly in the surviving prisoners' ears for the rest of their lives, and the traumatic treatment and torture they experienced would never leave their thoughts for a moment.

A great many of them refused to discuss their terrifying ordeal with even their close families, relatives and friends, or indeed anybody else. All they could do after the war was slowly but surely try hard and stoically to slot back into their usual day-to-day routines and family life. This must have been an almost impossible task for many of them, especially as there was no form of psychological support or therapy provided by the military or government to help them recover.

CHAPTER TEN

JAPANESE BARBARITY

The viciousness of the Japanese guards and officers was beyond belief and hard to reconcile, grasp or, indeed, fully understand. They would take great delight in aggressively dragging sick prisoners from their beds and forcing them onto the railway to do a full work shift even though they were in no fit physical or mental state to work. If a prisoner dropped with exhaustion, the guards would just kick and beat them mercilessly back to work on the railway. The brutality was so severe, as the railway was being built at such a rapid pace to meet the Tokyo Imperial Supreme Command's ridiculously ambitious completion deadline.

Johnny found this hard to witness, as his natural instincts made him want to jump in and retaliate, but he had to control himself in order to survive; if he lost control, that would be the end for him, or anybody else who tried to interfere adversely with the frenzied and urgent daily work schedule.

Nothing else mattered to the Japanese other than the swift and urgent completion of the much-needed railway at literally any cost to the prisoners' well-being or safety. The guards needed only the slightest excuse to strike a blow on any prisoner, and they would even lash out at some poor, unaware soul for no reason whatsoever, leaving him dazed and bruised.

This was all because the Japanese believed in prisoners having no real social status, as they had given up all their rights when they surrendered en masse in Singapore; this they considered dishonourable and weak. They could not accept that the prisoners had not fought to the death or killed themselves instead of accepting surrender and captivity from their enemy. This conduct was totally alien to their own way of life and their so-called 'noble' principles, even though, ironically, they surrendered themselves to the Allies in due course when the going got too tough for them.

The physical and mental state of the liberated prisoners after the Japanese surrender resembled a scene from the death camps in Europe. Their skeletal appearance was due to the savage and inhumane conduct of the Japanese army. On their eventual release after many years of torture, malnourishment and ill-treatment, prisoners were literally skin and bones, like walking skeletons. It is hard to reconcile this with their so-called principled and honourable code of 'Bushido', which the Japanese troops believed in so fervently and passionately. They proudly considered themselves to be a noble, principled, courteous, civilised people. This clearly contradicted the inhumane actions of their troops and the Imperial Supreme Command, with the ultimate countenance of the emperor.

The stories of human atrocities are numerous, widespread and truly sickening; they include many incidents of beheadings, torture, summary executions, rape executions and even human experimentation. There were also many other disgraceful, subhuman incidents of terminating the lives of the thousands of defenceless Allied prisoners of war and Romusha slave labourers in a merciless fashion. But one savage and sadistic case in particular, typifying the barbaric, animalistic and vicious bloodthirstiness of the Japanese, occurred in the railway camp at Kinsayok.

Chained to a wooden post, there was a wild monkey that entertained the prisoners. They would throw it the odd scrap of food, and it was treated almost like a camp mascot and pet. One day, as a prisoner gave it a minute scrap, a Japanese officer hit him in the ribs with the butt of his rifle, causing him to collapse on the camp floor in agony. The officer kicked him several times as he lay there and loudly ordered him harshly back into camp. He then turned to the monkey and with a swift swipe of his sword sliced off one of the monkey's arms. The animal screamed and screeched, writhing in agony, with blood pouring out from its gaping wound. The guard just stared and calmly and unemotionally walked off.

The alarming distressed squeals from the poor creature ran disconcertingly throughout the camp. The monkey was left in total agony, crying and whimpering in excruciating pain for several hours.

Then the same officer returned and sadistically sliced off the other arm, again smiling at the watching prisoners, who shouted various loud and angry obscenities at him.

The poor animal screamed and screeched, writhing on the chain, while the prisoners shouted more foul-mouthed obscenities at the guard, but he just walked off again, smirking and apparently very pleased with himself. He returned again a few hours later and put the dying monkey out of its lengthy misery by viciously slicing off its head with one swing of his gleaming sword.

This incident illustrates so graphically the evil streak that ran through the Japanese, from the lowest rank to the highest, and shows how relentless they were. This appeared to be a common characteristic among them.

One of the Japanese items of torture was the dreaded 'sweat box'. This was a metal container that restricted the movement of the prisoner so that he couldn't stretch out or even move in the sweltering 40-degree tropical heat. It was almost impossible to survive in one, as it caused the men to quickly faint and wildly hallucinate, and they could not get any sort of sleep.

The Japanese would find any excuse to incarcerate a prisoner in a sweat box and leave them there, isolated in the blistering tropical heat. They seemed to relish and delight in any form of harsh treatment towards the prisoners, even though many of them quickly died, thereby reducing their much-needed workforce.

It is somewhat ironic that a people who pride themselves on the principles of honour, civility and nobility treated their fellow human beings in such a ferocious, savage manner, with complete disregard to fair play, decency, mercy or sympathy.

Also, it is important to note that none of these dreadful atrocities are included in their current school curricula, so the young generation are completely oblivious to the barbaric behaviour of their troops during World War Two.

They also still honour and bow to several convicted war criminals at many shrines in Japan, like the Yasukuni Shrine in Tokyo, which celebrates and enshrines various war criminals from many conflicts, including World War Two. Indeed, many 'Class A' war criminals were enshrined at Yasukuni in 1978 in an attempt to glorify their militaristic past, even though they were found guilty of disgustingly horrific crimes against humanity.

It is repugnant the way a large element of the new generation and their religious leaders still try to excuse, and indeed honour, the unforgiveable actions of their parents and grandparents in the savage World War Two troops and the Imperial Command, many of whom forsook common decency and civilised behaviour for a twisted perversion of sadistic and frenzied nationalism. They should all be recalled with only great shame and sorrow, and certainly not with a shred of honour.

The Japanese nation is currently guilty of a convenient collective rejection of the historical facts, in spite of the overwhelming evidence that exists to substantiate the charges of torture, murder, execution, sadism and contempt for their military captives against all recognised honourable codes of conduct in modern warfare. It is clear and irrefutable that such a blatant denial still exists within the Japanese nation and that they have not yet come to terms with the horrors their troops inflicted on so many innocent people in their master's quest for global territorial domination.

When reflecting in his later years, Johnny once said, 'The real worry is that it may lay dormant in one generation, but it is even more concerning for humanity that the evil and barbaric streak may once again emerge sometime in future Japanese generations.'

CHAPTER ELEVEN

DEATH AND SURVIVAL

The main aim of each prisoner was simply to survive each day and hopefully be released and repatriated at some time in the future, if and when the Allies eventually triumphed. However, as the hours became days, weeks and then years, it became increasingly tough to get through the nightmarish ordeal. As well as the difficult mental strain, physical exertion and constant hard manual labour, they witnessed the deaths increase dramatically—with mass burials and cremations—while still having to adhere to the strict Japanese work schedule.

Disease was the main cause of prisoner-of-war deaths. The majority fell sick due to malnutrition, and Japanese guards refused to provide sufficient, if any, medical supplies to ease their discomfort and pain. Most of the prisoners suffered from more than one disease at a time, but only the critically sick would be excused from the frantic work schedule. Men who would have been considered seriously ill in civilian life had to continue working. Having said this, even the sick and dying were sometimes used to carry out basic chores like holding lamps as darkness approached.

Dysentery and diarrhoea caused more than a third of prisoner deaths; the continuous passing of watery stools led to dehydration and drained them of vital vitamins essential for their survival. The lack of vitamins due to a minimal diet also led to diseases like beriberi, which caused wasting and partial paralysis, loss of muscle function, vomiting and confusion. Also, the ubiquitous mosquitoes spread malaria to virtually every prisoner, and Johnny suffered with it throughout his captivity and on his return home. Malaria symptoms included chills, fever and muscle weakness that remained in the system many years after the war ended. Malaria accounted for nearly 10 per cent of all prisoner deaths.

One of many camp cemeteries.

Although tropical ulcers only accounted for around 2 per cent of deaths, the prisoners particularly loathed them, as even the smallest scratch would quickly develop into a gaping septic ulcer. The wound rapidly became infected by microorganisms that would eat away the flesh down to the bone. It looked as if a strong acid or a vicious animal had eaten its way through the pus-filled flesh to the bare bone. Often urgent amputation of the limb was the only real option for survival, but without proper medicine and surgical equipment, many prisoners did not survive the procedure and died.

Cholera had a high mortality rate and was extremely contagious; it was responsible for more than 10 per cent of all prisoner deaths. It was spread by food and water contaminated by faeces, particularly during the monsoon season when latrines (toilets, especially communal ones in a camp or barracks) overflowed. The symptoms of this dreaded disease were truly awful. With severe loss of fluid, cholera victims became unrecognisable within a few hours, and once diagnosed, they were housed like lepers in separate huts, or camps if possible, and name-tagged for identification later. The poor souls who died were promptly cremated. The Japanese guards feared the dreaded cholera even more than the prisoners did, and it was one of the only diseases they treated seriously and provided medication and anti-serum for, as required by the medics.

With numerous daily deaths during the height of the 'Speedo' period in 1943, each camp would have its own roughly laid-out cemetery. Medical personnel kept details of each gravesite so that bodies could be identified and hopefully recovered at a later date.

Funerals, which were actually permitted by the Japanese, were held with as much solemnity as possible as the acrid smell of the pyres and smoke drifted slowly across the camp.

The remaining 'fit' prisoners were mostly in poor physical and mental health even before they reached the Death Railway. The long arduous journey undergone by the Saigon Battalion further affected their health, despite the Japanese assuring them that the destination would be a lot easier for the than the Saigon Docks. The Japanese regularly made similar spurious promises to entice and cajole the prisoners, telling them there were better times ahead.

Survival rates differed greatly from camp to camp along the railway, dependant on the location, food availability, medicines, calibre of prisoners, and their officers. Camps located near running water had better sanitation, and those near local population centres had a better chance of obtaining food, and maybe medicines too, as well as a chance to trade items. In more remote camps the conditions were filthy and unhealthy. Prisoners worked on a starvation diet, and this exacerbated their health problems. These camps inevitably had the highest death rates.

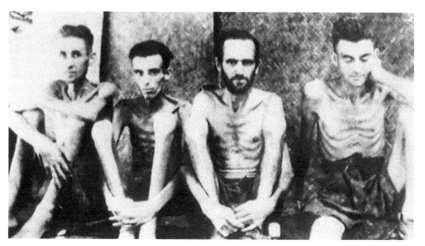

Weary and near-starving prisoners of War

Amid all this death, disease and deprivation, the prisoners had to try to remain reasonably sane and in control of their emotions. This was even harder than the punishing physical work, particularly during the night, when there was time to think and ponder about their awful predicament.

Their mental strength, or lack of it, undoubtedly affected their chances of survival. Many prisoners died because, due to their exhaustion and their emaciated state, they simply lost the will to carry on, preferring to give up on the punishing ordeal and fade away.

Life on the Death Railway was pared down to the two critical essentials for survival: nutrition and camaraderie. Almost all the prisoners relied heavily on camp friendships, exchanging stories and conversation. This literally meant the difference between life and death for some of them. Physical and psychological support was paramount for prisoner survival and gave the men the hope and drive to carry on in spite of their incessant nightmare.

Johnny's own solid willpower was helped by his cheeky Liverpudlian sense of humour. This also assisted his fellow prisoners throughout their torment and hardship. He was a strong and resilient character, who would help his friends whenever he could.

Comradeship and helping each other out was a critical element in prisoner survival; even just a kind word of concern or support gave a mighty boost to morale for the struggling men.

CHAPTER TWELVE

DISEASE AND DEPRIVATION

Although Johnny was a tough character, he succumbed to many virulent tropical diseases that greatly sapped his strength and stamina. However, he was determined to fight for his survival and focussed on staying alive and enduring each day, both mentally and physically.

After a few months in the Kinsayok Camp a large number of the battalion were moved to the Tarsao Camp. They were held there for another seven months, again working seven days a week from dawn till dusk and surviving on the usual starvation diet, with little medication or treatment. The pace of work was still relentless and tiring, with the usual 'Speedo' pace, and it was a real struggle to survive each day. Here, they were under the command of another officer: Lieutenant Colonel Knights.

Tarsao was a huge headquarters built in the shelter of the jungle, with roads that carried the Japanese troops and supplies to the Burma battlefront. These roads were badly rutted and always muddy, with trucks getting stuck regularly. They were completely impassable during the torrential monsoon season.

The first thing that caught Johnny's eye there were three large gloomy cemeteries. This did not bode well for the future.

There was a large fast-flowing river that occasionally gave the prisoners the opportunity to wash thoroughly and care for their badly swollen and sunburnt bodies.

Tarsao was supposed to be a hospital camp, but the conditions were primitive and truly appalling. The prisoners ensured their names were on the work lists simply to escape the rancid toxicity and acridity of the run-down camp and all its rampant contagious tropical disease and illness.

Burial ceremony

The so-called 'hospital' was poorly sited, close to the river, and accommodation consisted of just eighty-four badly constructed bamboo and attap huts in a desperate state of disrepair and virtual collapse.

The Japanese believed that if a prisoner was sick, he was useless to them and was better off dead, as they wouldn't have to feed him any more.

The prisoners often scraped together cash and valuables to trade with the locals on the river, who plied their trade with the guards and captives alike. Eggs were much sought after by the prisoners for their excellent nutritional value.

The usual meagre daily rations would consist of a small portion of rice and sometimes a piece of spoiled fish or meat, which was frequently contaminated with rat droppings and infested with maggots. Also, with minimal potable water, the prisoners were always dehydrated and predisposed to many tropical illnesses. This was compounded by the mud, slime and unsanitary conditions in the boiling-hot environment, which led to diseases of all types being rampant throughout the camp.

Cramped living conditions

Johnny and his fellow prisoners were crammed into the already-crowded attap huts with uncomfortable slatted beds that teemed with bugs, insects and lice.

There were virtually no medical supplies in this so called 'hospital' camp, and most of the prisoners had several debilitating diseases yet were still forced to work by the merciless Japanese.

The seriously sick were put in one designated hut where numerous men died daily. The others, apart from the cholera sufferers, were put in separate accommodation to those with tropical ulcers, as the acrid stench was sickeningly awful and extremely difficult to cope with.

Johnny worked day in day out, in spite of his illnesses, and his strong mind and determination carried him through the long back-breaking nightmare of forced labour.

The Japanese were particular about counting the prisoners twice daily to ensure there were no escapees. The first was the morning counting parade in the boiling hot sun; the other was carried out on return to camp.

After seven continuous months of slave labour in Tarsao, Johnny was moved to another railway camp in Tamuan. Here, he was again placed on the same daily grind of working on the railway from daylight to dark under the strict supervision of the bullying guards. He was there for another eight frightening months, suffering from disease, illness, beatings and minimal nutrition, which seriously tested even *his* strength. He sadly watched his fellow prisoners and friends dying daily, and he attended numerous solemn funerals at the various primitive cemeteries, which the Japanese oddly enough allowed to take place.

Even with his own strong willpower and mental strength, he began at times to doubt his own future. He wondered if this hellish nightmare of slave labour would ever end.

Not surprisingly, a significant number of Japanese prisoners of war suffered for many years after their release from captivity and continued to have numerous debilitating health problems. Anxiety, depression, flashbacks and nightmares affected at least a third of the men for many years. Recurrences of malaria and dysentery were also common in the post-war years, and there was an excess of death from tuberculosis and liver disease.

As stated previously, there was no counselling or therapy for post-traumatic stress disorder available to the men; they just had to 'grin and bear it' during the incredibly difficult post-war period.

CHAPTER THIRTEEN

NAKOM PATON

Johnny had now been a Japanese prisoner of war for nearly three years, working like a slave in Saigon and on the dreaded Death Railway. Eventually, the tropical diseases and incessant hard manual labour caught up with him. He was transferred, in January 1945, after a short stay at Tamajao Camp on the railway, to the infamous Nakom Paton Hospital, west of Bangkok.

On the journey there by train, which was uncomfortable, hot and noisy, Johnny was delirious from a combination of malaria and jaundice, which made him pass out constantly, leaving the other prisoners fearing the worst for him. Needless to say, the Japanese guards were not interested and completely ignored his serious and sorry plight, showing no sympathy.

The Japanese only sent to the hospital those prisoners who had absolutely no work value and were seriously sick. Nakom Paton was specially built to impress the Red Cross and was supposed to accommodate about 10,000 prisoners who were in desperate need of urgent medical attention.

Lieutenant Colonel Sainter was the administrative officer in charge of Johnny and his fellow prisoners confined to this hospital camp. He, along with other Australian and Dutch medical officers, would secretly have dealings with the Thai underground, who supplied much-needed medicines and updates on the progress of the conflict in Burma.

It was most ironic that visible from the camp was the gilded, towering Phra Pathon Chedi, which was the most sacred place in Thailand. This marked the site where missionaries from India first taught Buddhism in the Kingdom. It was once referred to as 'a symbol of civilised existence', so it was quite ironic that it was so close to the

Japanese hospital camp. This symbol of civilisation overlooked the tragedies of the Imperial Empire of Japan's inhumane policy of slave labour, torture, executions, killing and total disrespect for human rights and civilised conduct.

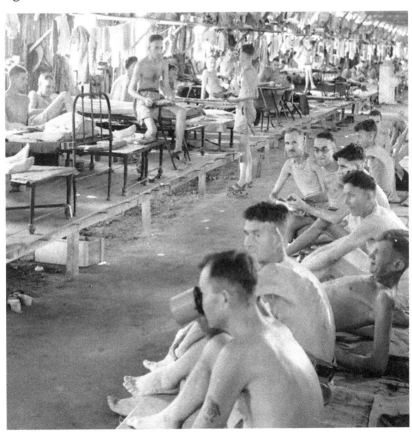

Hospital barracks

The camp had fifty fairly well-built huts with reasonable and sufficient latrines and was located about thirty-odd miles west of Bangkok. However, the sanitary conditions with regards to drainage were diabolical due to the hospital camp being built on some old, flat paddy fields. Consequently, when it rained the camp became a muddy swamp, with the roads and huts under at least a foot of thick muddy water. In the dry weather it was the opposite, with insufficient water even though some wells had been bored. The only real substantial water available to the prisoners was for cooking purposes.

The camp was divided into five sections: dysentery, surgical, anti-vitamin, general medical and 'fit.' There were only about 600 'fit' prisoners, who were used for camp work duties and various other chores.

The medical supplies were thankfully more plentiful there, with a much greater supply than in the railway camps, and the discipline, initially, was less severe, However, this did not last long!

Nakom Paton was a dismal place, with thousands of sick and dying prisoners striving for daily survival, and it was important for prisoners to rely on the support and spirit of their fellow captives to try to keep their spirits up in these awfully dismal and depressing conditions. A FEPOW patient once said, 'Without friends in Nakom Paton, a man must surely die.'

The days dragged into weeks, and Johnny gradually began to regain his strength and focussed on what was yet to come for him.

After a few months there, the Japanese suddenly declared urgently that they needed more 'fit' workers, and they formed a new convalescent block that drew from the other sick huts, excluding the 'fit' hut.

Slowly but surely, the hospital camp was transformed into a work camp, and the severe discipline began all over again, with the usual harsh beatings and brutal maltreatment along with more cries of the hated 'Speedo' by the frantic guards.

At this time the Japanese were getting nervy and worried as the Allied bombings became more frequent and a lot closer to the vicinity, with more regular sorties and fighter attacks taking place.

The Japanese started to form several work groups, and because the Allies were getting closer by the day, and gradually gaining the upper hand in the conflict, they decided that they needed a contingency plan—an escape route in case of full military retreat.

Also, the Nakom Paton hospital camp was gradually taking in more injured and wounded Japanese soldiers returning from combat on the frontline. They therefore reduced the number of huts down to only twenty for sick prisoners and used the rest for treatment of their own badly wounded troops. This gave the prisoners hope that the

Allies were getting nearer to them and that maybe the end of the war was a distinct possibility at long last.

In mid-April 1945 Johnny was selected to join a 1,000-strong force of so-called 'fit' prisoners to build a road through a thick, disease-infested virgin jungle. This was in case a retreat route was required by the Japanese troops, who were now being swiftly and steadily pushed back by the Allies. It was the start of another horrendous nightmare for Johnny and was to be far worse than the Death Railway camps, the Saigon Docks or the infamous Changi Prison. He would be extremely fortunate to survive this next awful chapter in his seemingly never-ending ordeal of Japanese captivity.

CHAPTER FOURTEEN

THE MERGUI ROAD NIGHTMARE

Prior to the Nakom Paton Hospital Camp being reduced in numbers, the Japanese demanded 1,000 'fit' men to come forward for duty, but only 500 of them were reasonably able, and even they were still struggling. The Japanese were furious and insisted that the remaining 500 should come from the 'least' sick. They insisted that if the Allied medical officers couldn't volunteer them immediately, the Nip Medical Officers would decide for themselves and inspect the men accordingly.

The sick men were paraded in front of the Japanese medical officers for assessment in rows of four, and if they could just about walk, they were considered fit for work.

Johnny had regained some of his strength, as the debilitating effects of his diseases had eased somewhat, so he was selected as one of the 'fit' prisoners for the upcoming urgent building project.

The 1,000 prisoners—about 600 British, 200 Australians and 200 Dutch—were marched in the tropical heat for nine long days and were told that they were heading for a base camp with easier conditions and far better food. However, little did they know that they were all heading to another dreadful ordeal, from which hundreds of them would sadly not return alive. The promised lighter conditions and better food, of course, never transpired and was just another Japanese lie to coax the men, giving them false hope and encouragement.

Unknown to the prisoners, the Japanese were being gradually and firmly pushed back from the Burma frontline by constant heavy attacks and bombing from the RAF and Allied forces. The Japanese generals were planning a full retreat but frantically and urgently needed a safe and practical escape route as soon as possible as a contingency plan before actually confirming the official retreat command.

The notorious Mergui Road was to be hastily cut at the junction of the Thai-Burma-Malaya border through dense virgin jungle across the extensive Kra Isthmus to Mergui, Burma. The targeted area, where the first 200 prisoners would cut and hack out a path about 3 yards wide for about 9 miles, was dense, swampy and mountainous. No food or medication was taken with them.

When this section was finally completed they slept in the jungle, on the open ground, exhausted and unable to carry on any longer. The following day they would commence the next 9 miles, hacking and chopping a further extended pathway through the jungle and the treacherous bug-infested swamps.

At the same time, the second group of 200 prisoners would leave the base camp carrying minimal rations and some basic medication

The first party were driven at full 'Speedo' pace for two days without any food, little water and hardly any sleep. The Japanese guards continued beating them and screaming at them constantly in their urgent drive to complete the task before the beginning of the forthcoming torrential monsoon season.

This relentless work continued until about 2,000 prisoners and Romusha Asian labourers, in groups of 200, were all doing the same thing under stringent and severe Japanese supervision.

In only six weeks almost 400 died in the jungle, over 700 were too sick to continue and 150 were returned to Nakom Paton Hospital Camp seriously sick and weighing only 5 or 6 stone, all from the hectic attempt to swiftly complete the new Japanese escape route.

Most of the native Asian labours (Romusha) either died during the rapid construction or ran off despairingly into the dense jungle, with no real hope or chance of survival.

The air was humid, and the tropical sun beat down mercilessly, like a thudding hammer, on the weak, exhausted prisoners and poor Asian labourers. They were covered in leeches, which clung to their emaciated skeletal bodies, sucking what little blood they could from the demoralised, starving captives. Clothed in just flimsy loincloths, they sweated profusely and walked uncomfortably and painfully in bare feet on bamboo thorns, rocks and bug-infested mud, slime and other sharp rubble.

Allied planes armed with cannon fire frequently attacked, zooming over the jungle, sending prisoners and guards alike scampering frantically into the undergrowth to shelter from the noisy spasmodic strafing, emerging afterwards badly bruised, scratched and greatly shocked.

There was very little water, and prisoners were lucky to get one dirty cup a day to survive on, so when they passed a stream, they would jump in to bathe and drink, not even caring whether it was dirty, harmful or disease-ridden. All the group camps on the road were infested with tropical mosquitos, bugs and lice and had an awful, putrid stench that filled the hot, stifling air. This made it almost impossible to sleep, and it was always an early start at daybreak, with the constant screams of 'Speedo' driving them on to work on the road.

The previous three years of punishing treatment and disease had worn the men down to exhausted, puny versions of themselves. Even Johnny had lost a substantial amount of weight due to the harsh work, malnutrition and tropical diseases. He was about 6 stone and was struggling along with his fellow prisoners, but his fierce sense of survival and strong disciplined mental focus just about kept him going from day to day.

As they approached the mountainous region of the proposed escape road, things drastically worsened for the weary prisoners and Asian Romusha labourers. Many of the men were extremely tired, collapsed through exhaustion and had to be carried along on makeshift bamboo stretchers together with all the necessary equipment. Some tottered and swayed and had to be helped by the few remaining 'fit' ones, who then bore the brunt of the remaining heavy workload themselves.

The mad, frenzied drive to finish the road at all costs made the whole situation seem unreal as the Japanese became more and more agitated and dealt more harshly with the men.

The prisoners and Romusha worked non-stop at the summit of the mountainous region in the surrounding thick, swampy jungle. With sweat dripping from their emaciated bodies, and being harshly driven by the ferocity and angry 'Speedo' cries of the vicious Japanese guards, this was truly a hellish nightmare.

It soon became obvious to Johnny and his comrades that this was indeed a one-way road for a planned Japanese retreat. It had had to be completed quickly, at least before the July torrential monsoons were due.

Although Johnny was struggling like everybody else, his love of manual work and self-determination made him focus on frantically felling trees, shifting and lifting large boulders, removing tough bamboo roots, and other tough manual tasks. These kept him occupied and mentally focussed, if nothing else.

He carried out his heavy manual chores while trying to help as many other struggling prisoners as he possibly could.

The old, battered picks and shovels and other shabby equipment and tools were badly dilapidated and got even worse each day, making the job even more difficult to complete.

Any unnecessary delays for whatever reason frustrated and annoyed the uncaring Japanese guards, who were now fully consumed with the arduous task of building the urgent escape road. They would continue to kick, beat and cajole their exhausted captives into working faster and harder, no matter what state of health they were in and without a shred of sympathy or mercy. They even began to keep the men working after dark, until they literally dropped and collapsed to the bare floor in a dazed slumber. The prisoners had to try to sleep as best they could on the bare, insect-ridden jungle floor. They were utterly exhausted and totally incapable of any more physical exertion.

The continuous layer of sweat on the prisoners' bodies left a thin film of salt glistening in the sunshine. This residual salt would attract a nasty assortment of inquisitive insects, like wasps, angrily buzzing around their tired exposed bodies. There was also, of course, the numerous black swamp leeches that feasted on and sucked blood until full.

Each day fewer and fewer men were on work duty, leaving the smaller groups to complete the full heavy work schedule by themselves. Even though there were fewer men each day, they still received the same brutal Japanese supervision and screaming frenzied orders of 'Speedo' till they themselves finally dropped with total exhaustion.

The meagre food rations also diminished rapidly, and the death toll thereby mounted accordingly. This caused an increased prevalence of malaria, beriberi, septicaemia and severe malnutrition, all of which were now abundantly rife throughout the group.

The Japanese continued to make spurious promises of more food and water as they frantically urged the men to finish the road before the torrential monsoon season.

Unbelievably, the road was actually finished and completed on time, in just under four months. This was truly an incredible achievement for the skeletal and undernourished prisoners and Romusha labourers. Considering the atrocious weather, terrain and lack of food, together with no footwear, clothing or decent tools and equipment, it is amazing that the project was actually completed to the tight work schedule.

The real shock came for the prisoners as the monsoons began in real earnest. The constant heavy torrential downpours turned the sloping road into a thick muddy quagmire that was virtually impassable and dangerous. This meant that the lorries carrying food and supplies could only drive up to the base of the mountainous slope, causing a long bottleneck. This frustrated the angry guards even more than usual.

The prisoners had to struggle down the dangerous slippery slope to get the food and supplies and haul them back to the top each day. This was an extremely dangerous task and very tiring, with only a few 'fit' men managing it.

The Japanese informed the prisoners that all the 'fit' men now had to remain to carry out, as required, further maintenance and upkeep of the road during the rainy season. They were also informed that they would not be returning to Nakom Paton as expected, which shocked and bitterly disappointed all the men, as they had expected to head back on completion. However, they were far too weak and in no position to resist this awful news. There was no medication for the many sick and ailing prisoners who were left to just rot and die in the camps along the newly built road. Even Johnny was in a wretched state of emaciation and wreaked with disease. He started to think that returning home to Liverpool was a far-fetched dream and unlikely to ever happen. For the first time his hopes started to fade, and he seriously doubted his own survival.

Then one day a sudden, unexpected turn of fate came to his rescue. He was selected by the Japanese *gunso* (sergeant) to return with other sick prisoners to Nakom Paton Hospital for urgent medical treatment, as his malaria was now giving him serious hallucinatory problems and he was in no fit state to carry on.

Johnny and a group of badly ailing prisoners started their long walk back down the mountainous slopes, stopping off at each camp along the road for much-needed rest. The catastrophic scenes they witnessed at each camp were truly heartrending.

The first camp was like a graveyard, with bodies lying all over the place, most just exhausted and sick, staring into space, covered with only dirty, infested rice sacks as they lay on the damp ground. The once-upright attap huts were now flattened, and the remnants of the camp were strewn about haphazardly in an untidy mess of scattered rubble caused by the air raids and strafing.

The men there were far too sick to be transported back to base, and they lay motionless, staring into oblivion and just awaiting their inevitable fate. This was the result of the torture these poor souls had endured over the last three and a half years, and this was to be their final resting place.

Johnny bathed in the stream and lay down exhausted and shivering from his recurrent malaria, which had now returned again with a vengeance. He lay there covered in an old rice sack feeling dizzy and delirious, half awake and just waiting for dawn to arrive.

The next morning, most unexpectedly, transportation arrived, and Johnny, still looking dazed and confused, was loaded not too gently onto an open-backed truck with other sick prisoners to go back to the hospital at Nakom Paton

They eventually arrived at the town of Khiri Khan to pick up a train to Nakom Paton, and some friendly local Siamese people gave Johnny and his friends bananas and other food items—for which they were so grateful—as they lay resting and exhausted at the railway station embankment.

The place was in ruins and had been battered by Allied bombing.

Here they heard the great news that the war in Europe was over, with victory to the Allies. There were also strong rumours of a full Japanese retreat from Burma, which gave Johnny and his friends great joy and their first real feeling of hope and optimism for their future.

They boarded the train for a long, hazardous journey, but shortly afterwards were followed by Allied fighter planes that were strafing and attacking overhead, frequently making the train stop as passengers hurriedly ran into the paddy fields for shelter. The noisy, frightening Allied bombardment came rapidly, and just as quickly went.

Johnny was still delirious and extremely weary on the long train journey, with his fellow prisoners fearing the worst for him. He woke up from his unconscious state with a sudden start in the Nakom Paton hospital, feeling dazed, confused, weak and extremely exhausted. He was now under 6 stone, and his once-powerful muscles and physique were replaced by a thin, drawn, emaciated, skeletal physique—a much weaker version of his former stocky frame.

The nightmare of the Mergui Road was now finally over for Johnny, and he prayed that hopefully some better times were awaiting him.

When the Japanese finally capitulated to the Allied forces, many of the Mergui Road working parties could not be found, neither on the road camps nor anywhere in the dense jungle. Those who were found needed urgent medical staff and vital supplies to be dropped immediately from the air to attend to them before they could be moved. Most of the poor souls were near to death due to starvation, disease and the maltreatment of the Japanese guards.

The true horror story of the Mergui Road is not as well known or as greatly documented as the Thai-Burma Death Railway, but it was just as terrible for the men forced to build it.

It was an absolute nightmare for the unfortunate, emaciated, weary prisoners and Romusha labourers who had to work on it and endure the violent treatment of the Japanese troops who set such a ferocious pace to complete the escape road.

The Japanese soldiers now started to realise that the war was turning against them and a retreat was their only realistic option. This was why they were so desperate to complete the Mergui Road in such a short, almost impossible, timescale.

It is ironic that the words 'retreat' and 'surrender' were so abhorrent and dishonourable to these subhuman troops, with their so-called 'principled' and 'noble' Imperial Japanese High Command requiring them to adopt and worship their own samurai-like Bushido code of honour in battle with a no-mercy policy to all prisoners. In the face of their own impending defeat by the Allied forces, they, with a few exceptions, hypocritically chose to do both without any compunction or hesitation.

A noble and civilised nation should surely not condone and allow their countrymen to commit the inhumane atrocities of their cold-hearted and merciless Japanese troops. They preached piously about honour, principles and nobility while their military consistently murdered, tortured, executed and brutalised innocent men, women and children. It was somewhat hypocritical of them to profess to live by a noble code that was forged by the Samurai warriors back in the sixteenth century, on an even earlier legacy from the tenth century, and includes eight ethical principles of equal importance:

1. Integrity
2. Respect
3. Heroic courage
4. Honour
5. Compassion
6. Honesty
7. Duty
8. Self-control

Virtually every one of these noble principles was broken by the savage Japanese troops and their Imperial High Command during World War Two.

Johnny would never forget his own and his fellow prisoners' nightmarish time in captivity at the hands of the vicious Japanese 'animals'. Neither would he forgive them for the rest of his life for his horrific ordeal.

CHAPTER FIFTEEN

JAPANESE SURRENDER

The cataclysmic and violent devastation and destruction of the first and second atomic bombs were detonated by the US Air Force on the cities of Hiroshima and Nagasaki.

On 6 August 1945 the US dropped the first atomic bomb over Hiroshima. Sixteen hours later the American president called again for a Japanese surrender and Russia declared war on Japan. The US, Britain and China all called for the immediate unconditional surrender of the Imperial Japanese Army, with the alternative being 'prompt and utter destruction'.

On 9 August 1945 the US detonated the second atomic bomb over the city of Nagasaki. This was another catastrophic tragedy for the innocent Japanese civilians, but it brought the Far Eastern war to an instant and abrupt conclusion when the emperor intervened and ordered the immediate acceptance of the surrender terms.

The timely end of the war in the Far East, without a doubt, saved the lives of many of the remaining prisoners of war. If the war had not ended then, either the various deadly diseases would have finished them off or the Japanese would have terminated them all to eliminate any evidence of war crimes. If the Allies hadn't been victorious, it is almost certain that all prisoners would have been exterminated, as they been elsewhere. There was actually an order in 1944 from the Japanese High Command in Tokyo to prepare for the 'final disposition' of all the remaining military captives. They instructed all prison camp commandants, in the event of a successful Allied invasion across the border, to liquidate the camps and leave no trace of the maltreatment and atrocities carried out against their captives.

This order was sadly carried out in many of the prisoner-of-war camps in preparation for an imminent Allied invasion. Allied prisoners in Thailand had been forced to dig many mass graves during the preceding weeks but were thankfully saved at the eleventh hour by the eventual Japanese surrender brought on by the awful events in Hiroshima and Nagasaki.

The Japanese had in fact already started retreating and falling back rapidly after the constant Allied air bombardments and shelling. The word started to spread quickly through the camps, and the prisoners started to believe that the Allies were now gradually winning the war at last.

Johnny and his fellow prisoners were still dubious though, until they witnessed a dramatic increase in the number of wounded Japanese troops arriving at the Nakom Paton Hospital Camp. Also, many thousands of retreating Japanese troops were now frequently passing through the camp in a full and frantic retreat.

Finally, the official surrender of the Empire of Japan took place on 15 September 1945 and brought an end to the torture, punishment and maltreatment of the surviving prisoners at the hands of the Japanese army, savage bullying troops who inflicted so much misery, torture, abuse and death on their unarmed, sick and defenceless prisoners of war and hundreds of thousands of innocent Asian Romusha labourers.

By the time VJ (Victory over Japan) Day arrived, more than 30,000 prisoners of war had died from starvation, disease and harsh mistreatment, both inside and outside the mainland of Japan.

Johnny had been only 25 years old when he was taken prisoner by the Japanese in 1942, and he was now 29 and soon to be liberated. Those four lost years would stay with him and haunt him for the rest of his life.

Sadly, the end of the war did not mean the end of the nightmare, as there were many more prisoner deaths to add to the already mammoth fatality toll. The lingering cases of disease, appalling sickness and tragic accidents during the course of the evacuation and the murderous reprisals of many rogue Japanese troops combined to add greatly to the overall daily increasing death count.

Those fortunate enough to have survived owed their lives not just to their own resources and amazing resolution but to the remarkable compassion and support of their fellow captives the dedication of countless heroic medics who worked marvels in such primitive conditions with minimal medication and flimsy equipment, saving countless lives with their determination and expertise.

For Johnny and many others, the end of the war came not a moment too soon. They were saved from violent reprisals and being used as human shields by the Japanese in the face of defeat. The abruptness of the war's end saved them from the awful fate of hundreds of British and Australian prisoners in Borneo, who were literally marched to their deaths in an effort to prevent their liberation and eradicate any trace or evidence of the unspeakable horrors they had been forced to endure for so long.

Johnny was still not completely fit and was receiving medication and treatment for his recurrent malaria, jaundice, and other tropical diseases. Even when he heard the news of the Japanese surrender he didn't get too excited because of his wariness and stoic sense of *que sera sera*. In fact, when his camp was liberated and the surrender officially announced by a senior British officer, he couldn't be bothered to leave his sick hut to greet the news; all the other excited prisoners were euphoric and lined up on the camp parade area cheering and whooping and hugging the liberating Allied troops with great relief and many a tear. Even when there was a visit from Lord Louis Mountbatten to meet the prisoners he couldn't be bothered getting off his bed. He was in no mood for going out to see the man who was the Allied forces' supreme commander, who in his opinion had left the captured troops to rot under Japanese tyranny. He just stayed on his bed thinking of what he and his friends had been put through for so long at the hands of people who relished sadistic behaviour, and with no real support from the supreme command of the Allied forces.

Lord Louis Mountbatten issuing the terms of surrender to the Japanese at Municipal Building Singapore, September 1945

Johnny's mind soon turned to home and once again seeing his mother, father, brothers and sister in his beloved Liverpool. He just wanted to forget the horrendous three and a half years of brutal captivity, but the disturbing memories would of course remain with him and haunt him for the rest of his life.

When he was feeling a little stronger, after a week or so following the Japanese surrender, Johnny was transported urgently by a Dakota plane to Rangoon, Burma, for a full medical appraisal. He was sent to a special prisoner-of-war hospital for urgent medical checks and physical rehabilitation before his long, much-dreamt-of homeward journey back to his family in Liverpool.

On arrival in Rangoon he was taken to the prisoner-of-war hospital, where he received much-needed medical treatment and regular nutrition, together with gentle physical-therapy exercises. This went on over several weeks, to get him in reasonable shape for the long journey home and live as near a normal life as possible. For the first time in many years he slept in a comfortable bed with clean sheets and was given healthy nourishment. He was happy to receive the kind attention and care from all the nurses and medical staff, who knew of the absolute horrors and trauma he had been through in Japanese captivity.

Eventually, when he was fit enough and had gained some much-needed energy, he was scheduled for passage on a homeward-bound ship. This vessel was part of a special fleet prepared and ready to repatriate all the Far Eastern prisoners of war back to Britain. The whole project was expertly organised by the Repatriation of Allied Prisoners of War and Internees organisation (RAPWI).

The ships were mainly destined for Southampton and Liverpool, and Johnny boarded his for the long, six-week sea journey back home via India to his family, who he had not seen or heard from in a considerable while.

The journey was monotonous and tiring, but he was fed with decent regular nourishment, and it gave him time to think long and hard about his and his fellow captives' harrowing ordeal. He was also very much looking forward to the prospect of returning to his house, old haunts and friendly local neighbourhood in Liverpool.

So many questions flooded his mind. What would Liverpool look like after the war? How was his family? Would he get a job? However, sadly, and unknown to him, another awful shock was awaiting him on his eventual return to his family home in Toxteth.

CHAPTER SIXTEEN

WHEN JOHNNY CAME MARCHING HOME

The prisoner-of-war repatriation ship finally arrived at the famous Pier Head in Liverpool, and Johnny took his first steps back onto home soil. That first step on land gave him a great thrill at being back once again in his own city, under the iconic Three Graces and the majestic ever-watching, famous Liver Birds.

There were only a few people there to meet the other prisoners, as celebrations of the end of the war in Britain were now well finished and long forgotten. Nobody was waiting for Johnny, as his family did not know his actual whereabouts, only that he had been taken prisoner by the Japanese. They had received no further news.

Likewise, he had not received family messages from home during his long captivity, as the Japanese, in their usual cruel fashion, had not allowed any letters, or even Red Cross parcels, to be passed on to the prisoners.

The first thing he noticed as he marched through the carnage was the devastation and destruction to the surrounding buildings and houses on the route home. The scattered rubble and debris worsened as he strode up to the south end of Liverpool, which was a good thirty-minute march from the ship.

Liverpool Docks before World War II

Merseyside had been the most heavily bombed area of the country outside of London, due to its critical role—being a key strategic naval base and home to various manufacturing companies—in the British war effort. Around 4,000 people had been killed, 10,000 homes destroyed, 190,000 houses damaged and 70,000 people made homeless in the Merseyside area during the relentless and devastating German Luftwaffe bombing blitz. More than 800 tons of high explosives and some 115,000 incendiary bombs had been dropped on the city and its surrounding area.

Many of the once-solid buildings had been either flattened, demolished or severely damaged by the constant bombings by the Luftwaffe on one of Britain's key ports during the blitz.

The south end of Liverpool was situated close to the River Mersey, and this area had felt the full brunt of the nightly bombardment, with thousands of bombs dropped from hundreds of German bombers.

There was devastating damage along the banks of the river, and all the surrounding areas, which included commercial properties, railway lines, churches, hospitals, schools and houses.

As he passed St Luke's Church, on Berry Street, which was now just a bombed-out shell of its former grand self and one of the most shocking vivid symbols of the blitz, Johnny was shocked by the sheer level of destruction. The church had been totally gutted by a powerful German incendiary bomb, but its outer shell still stood defiantly, as it does to this very day, as a stark reminder of the horror of war, as well as the defiance of the British people.

St Luke's Church after the Blitz

It was an eerie and unsettling feeling for him as he marched up to his old house, passing many more gutted buildings and bombed houses, where children played dangerously without a care, enjoying themselves in the crumbling war-torn dwellings.

When he reached his own street Johnny nodded politely said hello to his inquisitive neighbours as they recognised him despite his gaunt countenance and much thinner frame.

On a visit to the war-torn city during the conflict, Churchill once famously said, 'I see the damage done by the enemy attacks, but I also see the spirit of an unconquered people.' This typified the courage, defiance and fortitude of the Liverpool people during this awful time.

Johnny finally reached his own front door at 20 Upper Stanhope Street, Liverpool 8, and knocked solidly, albeit a little nervously and in emotional turmoil.

He was filled with mixed feelings of warmth, relief and excitement to see his beloved family after such a long time away.

Unfortunately, to his absolute dismay, his mother had died the previous week and was laid out peacefully in her coffin in the front living-room surrounded by the whole family.

He was stunned at this painful sight in front of him.

His father shook his hand firmly and hugged him lovingly, and his brothers and sister hugged him, crying with emotion. The whole family cried with joy to see their long-lost brother, even at this awfully sad time.

They were also concerned to see the dramatic deterioration in his physique and weight. His weight was down to about 7 stone at that time, with his face looking gaunt and drawn, despite the nourishment he had received in Rangoon and on the ship back home.

Johnny showed little emotion as he stood there, seemingly in a hypnotic state; he was shell-shocked at the sight before him. He just stared at his mother's still body as he was overcome by many flashbacks of childhood: memories of her looking after him with her warm, unforgettable smile. He also thought about how the Japanese captivity had cruelly deprived him of so many years that could have been spent with her before her passing.

He was flooded by a thousand questions from the sad but excited family.

His father sat him down gently and made him a cup of hot tea and some toast with jam, which had always been a favourite snack of his as a youngster.

After a while Johnny went upstairs for a much-needed rest. If the truth be known, Johnny was still in a numb state because of his Japanese captivity and the many debilitating diseases that had taken their toll on him, so finding his beloved mother deceased on his return was a hard psychological hammer blow. During the following week he literally just went through the motions in a virtual trance, attending the funeral and the subsequent boisterous wake. He was in a constant daze when listening to memory-jerking stories of growing up in the tough Toxteth area with his brothers and friends. Everyone lent him their warm support at this sad time.

Sadly, in those days there were no post-traumatic-stress tests or therapeutic counselling of any sort. The liberated prisoners were just left to get on with life as best they could. What a terrible position for Johnny to be in. Nowadays, when mental health is such a big concern and a popular topic of debate, this would be hard to accept. When you consider the physical and mental maltreatment he had suffered for nearly four years in Japanese captivity, it is hard to believe that he was just left to his own devices to deal with the trauma. This lack of support, empathy and concern for Johnny and his fellow FEPOWs at that time was a real shame, hence the name they were given: 'The Forgotten Army'.

This situation was a sad reflection on the times, and indeed of the whole system, which was typical of the general attitude towards returning soldiers. The fact that the repatriated FEPOWs just got on with their lives is an incredible testament to their courage, determination, mental strength, sense of duty and amazing fortitude.

Indeed, in hindsight, the lack of support for Johnny and his fellow prisoners was shocking, shameful and unforgivable. Without doubt, this is something that should not have been allowed after their awful psychological ordeal and vicious treatment.

Johnny was finally demobbed and left the army in May 1946 with an exemplary military record.

He returned home once again and settled back into 'normal' life as best he could, trying hard to put his frightful Far East ordeal behind him.

After a while he asked his dad to try to get him a job on the Liverpool Docks, which appealed to him. He felt that he needed to get things back to normal in his life and earn some money for himself and the family, and the docks were quite close to his neighbourhood.

His dad asked him if he was sure about this, as it was hard work and long hours.

Johnny replied with a knowing smile, saying that he was quite used to conditions a hell of a lot harder and with longer hours and no pay.

His dad stared at him for a moment, then laughed out loud when he realised his unintended faux pas.

His father put a word in with the powers that be, and Johnny started work as a docker on the Mersey waterfront. This involved loading and unloading ships from all over the world. It was a tough manual job in the bustling key port. Although it was hard manual labour, he enjoyed it, especially the heavy lifting and carrying.

The dockers would turn up early and congregate in the archaic work pens each morning, then the dock foreman would pick the required number of men to work on the ships that day, leaving the rest to go home until the next day. This was the frustrating pen system of dock work. This primitive system of employment was irregular, and being chosen depended on catching the eye of the pen foreman.

Johnny, however, was happy to at least be working, albeit casually and semi-permanently.

His new job initially brought back memories of the time he'd spent working on the Saigon Docks with the ill-fated Saigon Battalion. The haunting memories of his savage captivity continued to plague his thoughts regularly, particularly at night.

One particular week, several months later, a Japanese merchant ship arrived in the port to unload its cargo, which sent Johnny's into an uncontrolled fit of anger.

As soon as he became aware of the origin of the ship, he threw down his docker's hook and, in an outburst of angry exclamations peppered with many colourful expletives, refused to carry on working.

He was instantly called up before the Mersey Docks and Harbour Board bosses, who insisted he had to accept it and work on the Japanese ship or lose his job. If he refused, he would face the sack, but Johnny was absolutely adamant and stubbornly refused to do so, telling them in no uncertain terms to 'shove their job where the sun don't shine'!

The bosses decided to sack Johnny, but the Docker's Union took up his case and said they fully backed his decision and would call an all-out strike if they tried to sack him for his genuinely principled stance.

The management reconvened and duly capitulated, so Johnny was officially excused from working on this or any other Japanese merchant ship from then on.

Johnny was comfortable and content with the decision and continued enjoying his new life and work on the Liverpool Docks at its busiest time, during the buoyant post-war economic recovery.

He continued to work at the port for more than twenty years, living a full, active, happy life. He married his wife, Mary, and brought up a family of two sons, Mike and John, and a daughter, Patricia, with many grandchildren and great-grandchildren. He even attended and marched proudly in an ANZAC (Australian and New Zealand Army Corps) anniversary military parade with his younger brother Joe in Australia while visiting his nephew Joseph. Johnny and Joe were both then in their eighties and still going strong!

Johnny passed away, still physically and mentally strong, at the ripe old age of 89, in July 2005.

The harsh trials and tribulations of his early years were a testament to his bravery, courage and phenomenal mental strength, which were truly remarkable and inspirational to all who knew him or had the pleasure of meeting him. These qualities saw him through not only a tough upbringing, but also the horrors of a traumatic period of captivity under the bloodthirsty Japanese in the many prisoner-of-war camps at Changi, the Saigon Docks and, of course, the infamous Death Railway, finally finishing his unforgettable Japanese slave labour ordeal with his almost fatal experience on the Japanese escape route project at the frightening Mergui Road construction—perhaps the worst and most traumatic period of them all—until he was finally liberated and allowed to march home.

POEMS

WHEN JOHNNY CAME MARCHING HOME

Born in Toxteth the bleak Southend of the bustling port of Liverpool
Where the tough streets, deprivation and poverty were your only real
school

A large family struggling to survive weekly on no more than a mere
pittance
In a multi cultural tribal area with very little hope and not much of a
chance

He grew up always fighting getting in many scuffles, fights and spats
And was so good at it that he was selected to box for St Pats

His playground was right there on the hard cobbled street
Where he roamed and played in his little sore bare feet

His boxing prowess and reputation began to quickly grow
When the travelling circus invited him to join their Show

Last 3 rounds with him in the ring and win some much needed dough
But not many lasted the ordeal and they took many a hard blow

He joined the army as a mere boy to serve his country and the King
Where again he showed his superb boxing skills in the ring

An Army boxing champion he soon became
Even the top brass heard of his growing fame

Off to Scotland at Scapa Flo he was quickly dispatched
Where the embryonic plan for the SAS was initially hatched

After lengthy arduous training in physical combat techniques with his special forces crew
He was now ready for proper
military action and battle in the heat of World War2

But he got involved in a fight with two confrontational Officers in the Mess
Which caused both opponents a lot of pain, punishment and self inflicted distress

Summoned to the CO's office and asked to formally apologise
He blatantly refused to do so which began his own demise

Although his actions were rightly justified but perhaps a little too crude
He was told to formally apologise or get sent back to his regiment and be RTU'd

So back to his Royal Artillery Unit he was then sent
And then off to the Far East in Singapore is where he then went

This treacherous journey would not be nice for him and he would shed many a tear
Heading to an unimaginable taste of hell was this young tough Bombardier

Manning the heavy ack ack artillery and always alert and ready
The Japanese attacked Singapore and the onslaught was savage vicious and steady

After a bitter battle to see this vital strategic stronghold defended
The Allies parleyed a little and then sadly surrendered

First imprisoned and Ill treated in infamous Changi then taken by the sweaty and filthy hell ship Nisshu Maru to far away Saigon
Where life turned even more ugly and nasty and virtually unbearable for young brave Bombardier John

The Japanese were barbaric, sadistic and dealt out many cruel, brutal and savage knocks
And the two courageous , heroic and desperate escapees Baxter and Cassidy were executed on the Saigon Docks
 After many repetitive months of hard Labour in the boiling hot Indochina sun
It was off to the Siam/Burma Railway of Death which would be the end for some

A dirty Cup of filthy water and a small portion of unappetising maggoty rice
Working 7 days a week non stop on the railway was insufferable, punishing and a very heavy price

The inhumane Japanese were brutal, vicious, unfriendly and barbaric
And it mattered not a jot to them if you were fit, weak or deliriously sick

'Speedo speedo' they screamed and that was their continuous repetitive shout
And the prisoners toiled and slaved daily till they were all exhausted and worn out

A rifle butt in the ribs or a stinging knuckle smack across the jaw and face
Was the regular calling card of this evil, cowardly and bullying Japanese race

Torture, cruelty and unbearable pain with no hope made many men understandably cry
But even more so when they watched their brave sick and weary comrades one by one slowly die

Every day they had to blast through a thick mountainous tropical jungle area
Even though riddled with beri beri, jaundice, cholera dysentery and debilitating malaria

The Japanese inhumane brutality was nasty , vicious and callously mean
In the worst living conditions and depravity the weary prisoners had ever seen

One day a fight was arranged between an Aussie boxing champ and John
And the Japanese surprisingly allowed the men to set it up and get it on

Round after round encircled by the officers, prisoners and the watching Japanese guards
The two brave scrawny prisoners fought competitively with bruises, cuts and almost no holds barred

When one of them staggered and seemed to be gone
Neither would give in and bravely fought on and on

After 15 rounds of combat sweat blows and blood
The Japanese CO suddenly stopped the fight as only he could

He praised the two prisoners for being so courageous and brave
And told the rest to work much harder or be put in a grave

A day later after receiving a really heavy face slap from a Japanese guard
John retaliated defiantly, fiercely and punched him back on the chin real hard

Just as the Japanese guards were about to bayonet him after beating him enough
The CO stepped in loudly to stop and they immediately backed off

The officer said in the fight he was tough, courageous and very brave
But warned no more disobedience would be tolerated and he must work hard and behave

Eventually the Allies were victorious and the lengthy War was eventually won
And the Japanese torture, punishment and barbarism was thankfully finally over and done

He was sent for a full check up in a POW hospital in Rangoon
Dreaming of getting better and getting back home soon

It was a long sail back to Blighty and a lonely landing at The Pier Head
From where he walked to his home in Upper Stanhope St to find his mother was dead

Life had been very hard for Johnny and full of some very tough knocks
But he soon got a slightly easier job down on the Liverpool Docks!!

I am so proud, honoured and privileged to be the Eldest Son
Of a FEPOW Hero from Liverpool
My brave and lovely Dad John 🙏

BARBARIANS OF JAPAN

Some people say that Japan is a dignified country and full of nice people bowing to their knees
But there are some of us who know their history better and truly abhor the hypocrisy of actions such as these

A warrior race and great fighters is of course true and that we all know
Living by their "noble" samurai code of honour the so called Bushido

In WW2 their atrocities were truly barbaric and horrifically inhumane
Torturing their captives brutally and inflicting so much cruel unbearable pain

The Geneva Convention states how armies should conduct themselves and how in war and conflict to behave
Nowhere does it mention using prisoners of war as a labouring animal and put to work as a slave

With their banzai attacks and vicious marauding effective jungle fighting
Cowardly massacring thousands of innocent men, women and babies in The Rape of Nanking

It was horrific how they conquered and killed anything that got in their way
Then using prisoners of war as slave labour on the infamous Siam-Burma Death Railway

Men who took a banana or some extra rice just to try and survive
faced brutal torture and punishment and were very lucky to stay alive

They were battered, slapped, bayoneted, viciously punched and booted

In some cases like brave heroic escapees Baxter and Cassidy in Saigon
they were summarily executed

Treating fellow humans like animals with cruel deprivation and cruel
starvation
Is hardly the actions of a so called noble, principled and honourable
nation

Brave prisoners who were exhausted, dying and virtually just down
to skin and bone
Were shown no mercy by their Japanese captors so far away from
their home

Thousands were brutally tortured, beaten and many more died
Denied at the Tokyo Trials of course where the Cowardly Japanese
Officers all timidly lied

Supposed to be a nation of honour, principles and of course their
beloved Bushido
But abused and mistreated prisoners daily with their incessant
screaming cry of "Speedo, Speedo"

Slave Labour on the railway was a draining and brutal long daily ritual
With real tough physical tasks but on minimal nourishment for bodily
fuel

In the Red hot tropical Sun and a filthy bug infested thick dense jungle
area
Emaciated slaves working daily suffering with beri beri, cholera,
jaundice and debilitating malaria

Bodies full of septic ulcers and still beaten brutally black and blue
Feet full of pus filled blisters from the jungle floor covered with sharp
prickly bamboo

This onerous physical labour was punishing, arduous strength
sapping and real hard

Whilst doing their best and constantly getting slapped and kicked by every evil, nasty Japanese or Korean guard

So many poor prisoners died on the Railway carrying out their arduous daily heavy load
And it was even worse for them on the horrific construction of the infamous Mergui Road

They took extremely sick men from their hospital camp beds at Nakom Pathom
So they could get their cowardly quick getaway escape route ready and done

Blasting a way through sheer dense Jungle and mountainous rock
Working their Asian prisoners and POWs brutally who they would constantly abuse and mock

The majority died working through this unimaginable horrific tortuous ordeal
A few hundred survived on just a bit of rice and dirty water for a daily meal

The brutality and inhumane atrocities thankfully finally ended
When the Japanese gave in to the Allies and ironically surrendered

The survivors returned home with deep psychological scars and nightmarish memories
But would never ever forget the cruelty and barbarism of their vicious Japanese enemies

So don't talk to me about Japanese honour, nobility and BS Bushido
Just talk to the FEPOWS and their families if you really want to know

Hiding their history in schools from their new generation
Is not the actions of a noble and proud honourable nation

Hirohito ruled his Empire and thankfully he has now gone

But the memories of his barbaric troops inhumanity will still linger
on and on

This barbaric trait may now be laid dormant in the Japanese Nation
But always remember it could once again emerge from a future
generation.

My Dad survived his lengthy captivity as he was a very mentally
strong man
But many of his mates didn't make it thanks to the Barbarians of
Japan.

THE MERGUI ROAD

One thousand sick and exhausted prisoners were selected from the hospital camp for this arduous task
And why such cruel inhumanity by the Japanese you might rightfully ask

They needed a road through a mountainous jungle for a quick getaway escape insurance
But the gaunt, sick and emaciated POWs had very little hope or hardly a fair chance

The Japanese were desperate to get the job completed and swiftly done
So they took their slave labour from the POW hospital at Nakhon Pathom

The men were sick, dying exhausted and very weary
But the sadistic Japanese couldn't care less and made their lives even more punishing and scary

Day after day and hour after hour in the sweaty stifling unbearable tropical heat
They laboured like slaves with septic ulcers and deep cuts on their legs and their poor exposed bare feet

The terrain was rough and the work was real hard, tiring and in awful conditions not at all nice
Putting in more than 12 hours a day on a little boiled water and some measly maggoty rice

If a man collapsed because he was exhausted and desperately sick
The cruelJapanese guards would beat him viciously with a rifle butt or sharp bamboo stick

Without a care for their discomfort, illness and obvious distraught and sorrowful despair

The vicious Japanese guards would just shout "Speedo speedo"and wave their bayonets threateningly in the air

After many exhausting months of slaving and barbaric torture, cruelty and strife
The remaining FEPOWS were lucky to barely hold on to dear life

The road was finally finished and hundreds and hundreds had sadly not made it and died
The survivors would never forget the savage Japanese brutality as they witnessed the horrors with eyes open wide

The Japanese were delighted and proud of completing this virtually almost impossible task
But was it worth so many brave FEPOW lives you may well once again ask

Japan is today a nation so proud of its heritage of 'Bushido' courage and bravery
But what they did to the FEPOWS was cruel, barbaric and far worse than slavery

They may chose to ignore it and omit any mention from the educational curriculum in their schools
But trust me, my generation will never forget your atrocities to our troops so don't try and take us for fools

Your inhumane treatment of our loved ones was so barbaric, vicious and cruel
So let your young ones now know the real truth and teach it to them in school

Unless you apologise properly and admit your horrific and sadistic inhumane crimes

Your deplorable and despicable barbarity will never be forgotten until the end of times

My dad was a victim of your savage torture and sadism on the railway and also on the Mergui Road losing his friends and shedding many tears
But I will tell my son to tell his son and his son and his to keep the FEPOW flame burning for many many more years and years.

A Tribute to the Mergui Road dead and survivors

THE MASSACRE OF NANKING

War is such a horrific, brutal and very frightening thing
And a graphic illustration of this is the despicable rape and pillage of Nanking

In order to break the hearts, minds and spirit of the Chinese
General Iwane Matsui commanded the savage destruction of all his Sino enemies

They burnt most of the city and committed atrocities on helpless civilians men, women, babies and children
Killing 50000 male civilians, raping 20000 women and girls and sadistically killing or mutilating most of them

They also butchered 150000 male "war prisoners" during their reign of terror and psychotic rages
Killing so many innocent people of each gender, race and all ages

The Chinese government had regretfully fled leaving Nanking undefended
Allowing the rampaging Japanese force to pillage, loot and rape which their Generals condoned, allowed and intended

Chinese soldiers were summarily executed in violation of all the laws of war
Innocent civilians were killed, raped, mutilated en masse in a ritual of carnage that you can only abhor

This barbaric savagery carried out on defenceless men women and children was totally inhumane
And carried out by An Imperial Prince, Generals, officers and cowardly troops in their Emperors name

The massacre of Nanking was conduct beyond belief and so brutally sadistic

The actions carried out by the so called military troops and officers
was barbaric and beyond animalistic
The innocent Nanking citizens endured this massacre and atrocity
for many weeks which was truly appalling
While the Imperial Japanese Army killed, mutilated, raped in the
name of Emperor Hirohito's calling

Their commanders ordered them to desecrate the city like a
barbarian horde
Instructing them to massacre, rape, loot and destroy but the normal
rules of warfare to be ignored

The Japanese have still never apologised for this loathsome atrocity,
although many have asked, but alas in vain
Believing it was all just a part and parcel of the War and done in their
Emperors name

Prince Asaka escaped justice and was disgracefully granted immunity
because of his imperial heritage
While General Matsui was rightly executed by the Allies for his
conduct as the commanding Japanese savage

The Japanese will still not accept and some even deny this vicious,
sadistic and barbaric war crime
But the history books and descendants of Nanking will always
remember their barbarity till the end of time

They can talk about pride, principles and their beloved Bushido again
and again
But the Massacre of Nanking is on their Nation's history such an awful
stain

They can continue to politely ignore it and bow as low and as much
as they want
But their disgusting massacre of Nanking was an inhumane and a
truly depraved barbaric affront

BBC RADIO INTERVIEW WITH JOHNNY IN HIS EIGHTIES

This is an interview by the author, Mike Berry, with his dad, (Johnny), who was 82 at the time. The local BBC station asked the author to do it when Emperor Akihito was having tea with the Queen at Buckingham Palace in 1998. It was after the ex-FEPOWS had lined Pall Mall and turned their backs on Akihito as he was driven past to Buckingham Palace.

JB. Well, just think of it, daylight to daylight in bare feet and getting a bowl of rice all day long and in the red-hot sun getting just a little cup of water two or three times a day and the water had to be boiled for twenty minutes, account of cholera ... and they didn't give you time to let it cool ... It was all 'Speedo'. Everything was 'Speedo' ... and when you got back to the camp down the mountains ... most of the lads would be flaked out ... you even had to go, those of us who had the willpower—I wouldn't say strength because none of us had any strength—would go down and get water, boil it and try and get the men, most whom were unconscious, to drink the water because you knew if they didn't drink the water, they would die.

MB. Was the work on the railway during the day very, very physically hard?

JB. Very arduous. Very, very hard. Can you imagine a rock? You empty all the soil off the rocks, leaving the bare rocks ... then you get a metre bar between two of you every two yards for about three or four hundred yards ... and you slogged this metre bar in. Now, if *you* tried to do it, you could never get that metre bar in right down to the metre mark because there was a knack in it. You had to keep turning the bar, otherwise the powder would just congeal. You have to take the powder out every so often with a little like a clam cork on a bit of wire, otherwise you would never get to the bottom! One man would use the hammer; the other man would hold the bar ... Many times you hit one another's arms and hands ... and a lot of times we had malaria ... and malaria is like as near as I can say is like a form of drunkenness

... You don't know what you are doing ... You think you are but you are not ... It would take four, five or six hours. That's how long it would take you to get the metre bar down ... and then when we got to the right depth, you would pull the metre bar out and the Japanese would put the TNT in ... but they didn't give you much chance to get away before it blew all the mountain up ... Many a time you were just down below and you had to put the *chungkols* over your head to stop the blowback coming down on us ... clatter, clatter, clatter ... and that's how they did it every three or four hundred yards ... and then you would have to go back up, in your bare feet of course, and clear all the shattered rock for about 5 metres because this was going to be the railway.

MB. What state were you in? Were your feet cut and your body covered in sores, or what state were you in physically when you were doing this work?

JB. Well, we were cut, and we used to get thorns in our feet because in this area there was bamboo growing and you often got bamboo thorns in your feet and you had to be very careful because once you got a cut in your feet, the next day it would be a big ulcer with the flesh open right down to the bone. You would never dream that this could happen in only twenty-four hours!

MB. How long were you working on the railway?

JB. About twelve months.

MB. In every week of the year, or did you get breaks?

JB. No, we worked all the time, day in and day out ... They couldn't get the railway finished fast enough ... It was 'Speedo ... everything was 'Speedo'.

MB. What time did you start in the morning, and what time did you finish at night?

JB. As soon as it was daylight in the morning we were on our way up the mountain, at about 7.30 am, I'd say ... and you would work up there till it was going dark ... when you left the job and came down the mountain back to the tent where you slept in it was dark ... They never lost a minute of daylight.

MB. Then you slept?

JB. No, first of all you had to get bits of wood to light a fire and then get some water from the river to boil, otherwise you wouldn't survive ... the drink you got during the day wasn't enough ... Quite a number of the men were too exhausted to even do this, so it was important for one or two of us to have the willpower to do it and keep going, because the other fellas would be all spark out.

MB. Where did the cruelty of the guards come into it. So far you have not mentioned the guards. What did they do? Did they knock you about?

JB. They would use the rifles on you for no reason whatsoever many times and jab and push the butt into your ribs ... and they used to use bamboo canes that used to split and cut you ... and they always used to hit you over the head.

MB. If any of the prisoners fainted because of the heat on the railway what happened?

JB. Oh they just kicked them ... they didn't give them any mercy, just kicked them till they come around ... They didn't give anybody mercy ... There was no use falling sick or anything ... they didn't worry about that ... they would just kick you ... As a matter of fact when they were short of men, some dying men had to go on the railway to hold lamps even though they were dying.

MB. Did any of the men retaliate, and if so, what happened?

JB. The only time I saw a man retaliate was in Saigon before I came to the railway ... This Japanese hit him with a rifle, and the man socked him and, of course, they got him and he went down and they battered him ... He died not long afterwards through the beating.

For the full interview recording please go to the link.

http://www.fepow.org/john-berry.html

Milton Keynes UK
Ingram Content Group UK Ltd.
UKHW022259170823
427026UK00015B/546